China Currents

2010 Special Edition

China Currents

2010 Special Edition

Penelope B. Prime and James R. Schiffman, Editors

China Research Center, Atlanta, Georgia
www.chinacenter.net

Cover design: Vanessa F. Garver

For electronic browsing and ordering of this, and other China Research Center titles, visit www.chinacenter.net

For more information, please contact:
China Research Center
Atlanta, Georgia
+1 (678) 547-6235

China Currents: 2010 Special Edition
Penelope B. Prime and James R. Schiffman, Editors

ISBN: 978-0-9826415-0-7

Published in the United States by China Research Center

Design and Production: Carbon Press LC
Manufactured in the United States of America

First Edition

Contents

China's Emerging Consumer Market

The Evolution of Business

Social Progress and Challenges

Preface

Economic reform and development in China are reshaping the global system in the 21st century and bringing about an unprecedented social transition within China itself. *China Currents* is a forum for thoughtful, concise articles that inform readers about what is happening in contemporary China. While *China Currents* is published as an online journal at www.chinacurrents.com, this special printed edition includes selections from past issues. This set of articles provides a broad survey of change in China based on academic research and the experience of practitioners.

China Currents is published by the China Research Center at www.chinacenter.net. The Center would like to gratefully acknowledge financial support from Womble Carlyle Sandridge and Rice, PLLC and East West Manufacturing, LLC. We would also like to thank Vanessa F. Garver, Jennifer Duckworth and Don Hoyt for their help in preparing the manuscript for publication. The views expressed in these articles are those of the authors.

Founded in 2001, the China Research Center's mission is to promote understanding of greater China. The Center draws much if its expertise from the universities and institutions around the southeast region of the U.S., working collaboratively and jointly with the public and private sectors. The universities represented include Agnes Scott, Dalton State, Emory, Georgia Institute of Technology, Georgia State, Kennesaw State, Mercer, Oglethorpe, the University of Georgia and University of North Carolina, Greensboro. The Carter Center also is a collaborative partner.

The associates of the Center believe that favorable U.S.-China relations will be critical to supporting economic development in the U.S. and greater China, and to promoting peace in the region. One of the foundations of favorable relations is mutual understanding based on knowledge and open communication. The associates study various aspects of Chinese language, culture, history, politics, society, international relations, demographics, geography, the environment, the economic system and the business environment. The Center's goal is to make knowledge and expertise available to a wide variety of constituents within and beyond our academic communities, as well as to enhance our academic work via cross-disciplinary and cross-institutional collaboration.

Penelope B. Prime
James R. Schiffman
July 2010

China and the Iran Nuclear Question

John Garver
Vol. 8 No. 3
Fall 2009

China is walking a tight-rope in handling the 2009 Iran nuclear crisis. On the one hand, Beijing's overriding strategic interest is to ensure a favorable "macro-climate" for its highly successful post-1978 development drive by maintaining good relations with the United States. Beijing realizes China-U.S. relations could sour if Washington begins to view China as a peer competitor, and that confounding U.S. policies in the Middle East could easily lead American leaders to such a dangerous conclusion. China's leaders also recognize the advantages accruing to China from a U.S. invitation to partnership on global issues. Viewed broadly, such a partnership might allow China's power to continue to grow without collision with the reigning paramount power – rather like the U.S. did in relation to the British Empire circa 1900.

On the other hand, Beijing is loath to forgo opportunities to expand economic and political cooperation with Tehran. Iran is one of the world's largest oil exporters, has large untapped reserves of oil and gas, and is a reliable supplier of energy for China. Moreover, China's energy security policies attempt to encapsulate foreign energy supply relations in a warm, political insulation. Iran also has a large demand for infrastructure of all sorts: industrial and transportation machinery and equipment, cheap consumer goods – all of which China is happy to supply. Iran's conflicts with the West have allowed China to establish itself as Iran's leading trading partner. (Before Iran's 1979 revolution, China supplied less than one percent of Iran's imports.) Beijing also recognizes Iran as a major regional power with no conflicts of interest with China (unlike India, Japan, Russia, or Turkey). Beijing's political objective is to expand China's influence with Iran into an all-weather partnership similar to the one China enjoys with Pakistan. This objective would be undercut by China ganging up with the United States and Europe against Iran over the nuclear issue.

China balances between these conflicting but weighty sets of interests. In the International Atomic Energy Agency Board of Governors and U.N. Security Council debates over Iran's nuclear programs, Beijing has endorsed efforts to negotiate a solution with both sides showing flexibility in order to reach an agreement that upholds the Nuclear Nonproliferation Treaty. This formulation implicitly criticizes both Washington and Tehran – Washington for trying to abridge Iran's "right" as a signatory of the NPT to the "peaceful use of nuclear energy," and Tehran for not adequately demonstrating to the "international community" that Iran is not attempting to make nuclear weapons. China is unlikely to thwart a new push by Washington, Paris, and London (Germany is unlikely to go along) to have the Security Council endorse a new and broader— "punishing" is the word used by U.S. representatives—set of sanctions. But China's words suggest that at the end of the day, it will not permit the Security Council to endorse, or itself participate in, tough economic sanctions against Iran. Rather, Beijing is likely to water down any sanctions to allow China's rapidly expanding economic relations with Iran to continue unimpeded growth.

Chinese analysts were deeply skeptical about the newly inaugurated (January 2009) Obama Administration's policies toward Iran. Efforts by the Obama Administration to improve relations with Iran had some effect, according to an August article in *China Daily* by the director of Jiangsu's Institute of International Relations. Yet despite a few moderate words and gestures by the Obama administration, Washington was likely to revert soon to a hard-line approach, which would fail, according to the article. "The long strained Iranian-U.S. ties have improved to some extent after Barack Obama assumed the office of the U.S. President," the article noted. But once "the world's largest economy bottoms out the Obama administration will [resume] its attack on Iran's nuclear program once again, increasing the pressure on Tehran." U.S. policies toward Iran continued to be "prejudiced." "An improvement in U.S.-Iranian ties depends more on the length Washington is ready to go to engage Tehran in a dialogue."[1]

Another *China Daily* article reviewing the demonstrations in Tehran protesting irregularities in the June 2009 Iranian presidential election was implicitly critical of U.S. "interference in Iranian internal affairs." The "international community" should not "add fuel to an already burning issue" by interfering in Iran's internal affairs, the article warned. An "attempt to push the so-called color revolution toward change will prove very dangerous" because "a destabilized Iran is in nobody's interest if we want to maintain peace and stability in the Middle East and the

---

1 Liu Qiang, *"Ahmadinejad has a real job on hand,"* China Daily, 13 August 2009, p. 9.

world beyond." President Obama had indicated, the article said, in his speech at Cairo University and in comments made while meeting South Korean President Lee Myung-bak, that the U.S. would not intervene in Iran's current post-election turmoil. The crux of the issue, the article implied, was whether the United States would adhere to these promises.[2]

China's opposition to efforts to accomplish regime change in Iran dovetails with China's own interests – or actually, with the interests of the Chinese Communist Party that has ruled China since 1949. CCP leaders well understand that the United States and other Western democratic countries believe that values of individual freedom are universal and give unique legitimacy to institutions of liberal democracy. Marxist-Leninist, Communist values and political systems are fundamentally illegitimate, according to this Western perspective, and Western governments are often tempted to apply these ethnocentric prejudices (in the CCP's view) to China. These Western prejudices, "Cold War mentality" in the CCP's preferred nomenclature, were directed against China during 1989-1994, culminating in U.S. threats to withdraw China's Most Favored Nation status (and thus severely restrict China's exports to the U.S.) unless China implemented major improvements in China's "human rights."[3] China's tough stance defeated that earlier U.S. effort, but events in Tibet, Xinjiang, or elsewhere in China pose perennial opportunities for renewed U.S. and Western "interference in China's internal affairs." CCP rule of China will be safer and more secure if Western countries abandon universalistic ethnocentrism and accept the reality of diverse political systems around the world, according to the Chinese view.

Beijing has consistently opposed imposition of sanctions against Iran – over the nuclear issue or any other issue, for that matter. It eventually voted in the Security Council for sanctions resolutions: No. 1696 in July 2006, No. 1737 in December 2006, No. 1747 in March 2007, and No. 1835 in September 2008. The sanctions authorized under these resolutions were limited to 28 or so individuals and entities involved in Iran's nuclear or ballistic missile activities. China, together with Russia and Germany, worked to ensure that those sanctions did not have much bite. Agreeing to vote for sanctions placated Washington, but watering them down ensured that Washington's quarrels with Tehran would not too adversely affect Sino-Iranian ties.

As the Obama Administration began to lay the groundwork for tough Security Council-sponsored sanctions should the 1 October negotiations with Tehran fail, Beijing made clear it thought such sanctions were a bad idea. A Xinhua article written by an international observer made clear that sanctions were a Western

---

2 *"For Peace in Iran," China Daily, main editorial, 18 June 2009. http://www.chinadaily.com. cn/opinions/2009-06/18/content_8296115.htm*

3 *From mid 1993 to mid 1994 the Clinton Administration demanded that China fundamentally improve its "human rights" situation or face loss of Most Favored Nations status.*

idea. "Western countries led by the U.S. have asserted that the real intent of Iran's nuclear program is to possess nuclear weapons," and "the Western countries have applied pressure on Iran in all forms in an attempt to force Iran to stop its nuclear programs." Iran had rejected all such pressure. Once again, in 2009, it was likely that "the United States and the EU" would press for a new round of sanctions against Iran. "However, because every country proceeds from its own interests, it will not be easy [to secure] the adoption by the U.N. Security Council of a resolution on imposing substantive sanctions on Iran."[4]

A Ministry of Foreign Affairs spokesman speaking on 24 September said that imposing sanctions and exerting pressure would not be "conducive to diplomatic efforts" to resolve the Iranian nuclear issue. "We hope that all relevant parties seize the current favorable period, step up diplomatic efforts and push forward the achievement of positive results," the spokesman said.[5] The proper paths were talks, dialogue, and negotiations, without a background of threatened force or sanctions.

As Western companies pulled back from Iran because of greater political risk in servicing that market, Chinese companies seized the opportunities to expand. In July 2009, the Iranian embassy in Beijing announced that China had become Iran's number one trading partner.[6] By seizing the opportunities created by Western problems with Iran, China pushed its way into a very large, lucrative, and growing market.

An embargo of gasoline was one "tough sanction" widely discussed in Western media. Perhaps in response, British Petroleum and Reliance of India stopped selling refined petroleum products to Iran in mid-2009. Total of France indicated a willingness to follow suit, should the Security Council so mandate. Chinese firms stepped in to meet Iran's shortfall. Chinese officials denied that China sold gasoline to Iran, but foreign analysts concluded that between 30,000 and 40,000 barrels a day of Chinese refined petrol was reaching Iran via third parties.[7]

Iran supplies large amounts of oil to China—typically ranking among the top three suppliers to China. China's energy security strategy stresses involvement in upstream foreign oil production, and Western sanctions against involvement in Iranian oil-development projects make Chinese participation attractive to Tehran. Iran also produces lots of mineral ores that China needs: copper, sulphur, zinc, chromium, iron, lead, and aluminum. Iran also offers excellent opportunities for

---

4 Liu Gang, "CPRC: Xinhua Stresses Dialogue in Settling Regional Nuclear Issue," Xinhua, 13 September 2005.

5 CPRC FM Spokesman: Sanctions "not conducive," 24 September 2009. Xinhua.

6 Ariel Farrar-Wellman, "China-Iran Foreign Relations," 26 July 2009. http://www.irantracker. ort/foreign-relations/china-iran-foreign-relations

7 Spencer Swartz, "Big Oil Traders Cut Shipments to Tehran Amid Sanctions Talk," Wall Street Journal, 24 September 2009, p. A4. Javier Blas, "Chinese companies supply Iran with petrol," Financial Times, 23 September 2009, p. 1.

Chinese exporters of transportation, construction, mining, manufacturing, and power-generation equipment and machinery. Iran has ambitious development objectives and adequate financial resources to pursue those objectives. Chinese machinery is not as technologically sophisticated as Western or East Asian (Japanese or South Korean) varieties, but Chinese goods are typically substantially cheaper, and quite good enough for Iran. Iranian engineers and manufacturers might, ceteris paribus, prefer Western or Japanese goods. But low political risk associated with Chinese goods in contrast to the risk of interruption or interference associated with Western goods (along with low Chinese prices) often trumps those Western advantages. Iran is a very big market, and Western sanctions offer Chinese firms an opportunity to expand into that market.

Iran's abrupt admission in late September 2009 of the existence of a second uranium enrichment facility inside a Revolutionary Guard military base at Qom will not significantly alter China's calculus. Beijing will want to stay in step with Russia in dealing with the Iran nuclear issue. Russia's calculations regarding Iran seem to have more to do with humbling the United States than do China's, and it seems unlikely that Russia will go along with a U.S.-led Western effort to enforce strict sanctions against Iran. Should this assertion prove to be wrong and Russia decides to go along with Western sanctions against Iran, China would probably follow suit. Without its Russian partner China would be uncomfortably positioned as the sole, major opponent of U.S. policies. At the same time, however, Beijing would insert as many loopholes as possible into the Security Council-mandated sanctions regime, and would find occasion for words and actions supporting Iran in the face of what Chinese media would certainly style "U.S.-led Western sanctions."

China's balancing act in the Security Council reflects two important but contradictory sets of Chinese interests that Beijing must accommodate. Economic interests weigh heavily in China's calculus, but strategic calculations are important too. China's interests would not be injured if U.S. efforts to lock Iran into a militarily inferior position (i.e., without nuclear weapons) collapses. U.S. prestige would thereby be substantially diminished. China's security against a possible hostile cutoff of China's sea-borne oil imports (either by the United States or India) would also be enhanced by having a friendly, militarily powerful and confident Iran willing to work with China to counter such hostile moves. China's leverage with Washington would also benefit from Washington finding itself in a long term political-military confrontation with Iran. The United States – and for that matter, Iran – would need China's assistance on various matters, while the U.S. would be less inclined to focus on East Asian issues closer to China's own vital interests. One Chinese analyst may have alluded to the primacy of such Chinese interests when he noted that, "Because every country proceeds from its own interests, it will not be easy for the United States to press for the adoption by the U.N. Security Council of a resolution on imposing substantive sanctions on Iran."[8]

In the dominant view among China's Middle East specialists, the root cause of the clash between Iran and the West has been the arrogant, bullying, and ethnocentric policies of Washington over the administrations of half-a-dozen presidents. It is American policies of sanctions, military strikes (during the "tanker war" of the 1980s) and threats, subversion, and no diplomatic relations that have, in Beijing's view, created the current morass and possibly pushed Iran toward nuclear weapons to defend itself. The United States is now stewing in the mess it has itself made – in Beijing's view. Why should China ignore its own interests by aligning with the United States against Iran? Even if Iran acquires nuclear weapons, China has no allies or military forces in the region that would be threatened by those weapons. Nor has China undertaken (unlike the United States) to guarantee the flow of oil through the Strait of Hormuz. China's general, and genuine, interest in limiting the number of nuclear weapons states is balanced against these multiple and major strategic interests.

But China must pursue these strategic and economic interests without injuring an even more important interest in maintaining cordial relations with the United States. Since 1978 China's drive for economic development has been underpinned by the imperative of maintaining friendly ties with the United States and, thus, a generally supportive American attitude toward China's development. This imperative continues to operate. It has been paralleled since 1997 by a U.S. push for increased strategic partnership with China in managing the affairs of the post-Cold War world. This U.S. policy creates a very favorable environment for the growth of Chinese influence, and Chinese leaders recognize many advantages from accepting U.S. invitations for strategic partnership and cooperation. This means that Beijing will not block U.S. moves regarding Iran in the Security Council and will cooperate with Washington at least to the degree judged necessary to keep Washington from viewing Beijing as a rival or competitor – much less a hostile power. Exactly what that degree entails will be determined by the estimates of Beijing's diplomats and analysts about the intensity of U.S. demands and the correlation of forces balanced behind and against Washington's moves. Beijing will probably cooperate with Germany and Russia to water down further sanctions. But Beijing will be loath to take the lead in opposing U.S. policy thrusts.

John Garver is Professor of International Affairs in the Sam Nunn School of International Affairs at Georgia Institute of Technology, Atlanta, Georgia.

---

8 *Liu Gang, op cit.*

2009: A Year of Audacious Hope or a Year of Utter Hopelessness?

Yawei Liu
Vol. 8 No. 2
Winter 2009

As 2008 ended and 2009 dawned, China seemed poised to move into political and social normalcy. The previous year had been filled with unprecedented challenges, but 2009 was supposed to be fun and festive, a period for enhancing legitimacy and consolidating national pride. Many believed that China would lift restrictions that had been tightened in 2008. International conferences would be held. Foreign and domestic NGOs would be allowed to operate with less harassment. Sensitive anniversaries would pass without major campaigns of repression. Yet, even before entering the New Year, there were signs that such a rosy scenario would not come to pass. From top Chinese leaders to main state media outlets, there were dire warnings that 2009 would pose an even more serious threat to China's stability. Chinese themselves were confused. China watchers were clueless. Where exactly does the threat come from?

It's the economy, stupid!

For starters, there is the massive economic downturn that has laid off no fewer than 20 million Chinese migrant workers. There is also the concern that millions of past and current college graduates will not be able to find steady jobs. Urban Chinese residents who live below the poverty line or have no unemployment benefits are being pushed deeper into misery. Restless migrants teaming up with well educated students have been the source of dynastic changes throughout China's history. Furthermore, the legitimacy of the Chinese Communist Party (CCP) has been built on the claim that under its strong leadership, living conditions of the

Chinese people have been on a 30-year rise. Economic devastation always generates anger and protest, but under China's circumstances, it also can pose serious political challenges for the Party.

Don't you see Westerners are pulling the strings?

Sensitive to China's political fragility and mindful of precedents set by Eastern European counterparts like Václav Havel, two Chinese dissidents drafted Charter 08, calling for the CCP to launch political reform in a meaningful way, including conducting elections, expanding freedom of speech and association, institutionalizing judicial independence and introducing a system of checks and balances. To the surprise of the government, Charter 08 was signed by many ordinary Chinese citizens despite the government's Herculean effort to cleanse the Internet of all traces of the document.

While chasing and talking to those who have signed Charter 08, the Chinese government is also busy identifying the instigators. Targets are easy. Evil Westerners who are jealous of China's enormous economic achievements and frustrated by Beijing's capacity to absorb social and political shocks are the culprit. Not only were they funding the Charter 08 endeavor, they were also behind the taxi drivers' strike and were trying to penetrate China's trade union groups. At the recent annual sessions of the National People's Congress and Chinese People's Political Consultative Conference, there were calls from the deputies to increase jamming of Western broadcasting into China.

His Holiness is not holy at all

In this volatile climate, there are many anniversaries falling in 2009 which are adding fuel to the gathering conflagration and making the CCP more nervous. The first date on the calendar is the 50th anniversary of His Holiness Dalai Lama's failed uprising against the central government. While Tibetans in exile commemorate the date on March 10, the Chinese government has changed it to March 28 and labels it as Serf Emancipation Day. All measures seem to have been taken to prevent the protests and riots that happened last year. Frustrated by what he sees as indifference and complicity, and forced to pacify the more radical members of Tibetan Youth Congress, His Holiness accused the Chinese government of "transforming Tibet into hell on earth" and extinguishing Tibetan culture and heritage. This will only harden the CCP leadership, blocking all possible channels of communication and efforts to restart negotiations aimed at creating a more autonomous Tibet within the realm of mainland China.

April is no fool's month

Ten years ago, tens of thousands of believers of a faith developed by an ex-policeman, Li Hongzhi, surrounded Zhongnanhai, where the central leadership lives and works, and demanded official recognition of their belief. Surprised and humiliated by the effective and secret organization of the demonstration, the CCP eventually labeled the group as a cult and launched a nationwide crackdown. Falungong believers can no longer practice openly in China but they are doing very well outside the country, using low-tech (cultural performances and newspapers), high-tech (satellite jamming and web sites) and polemic (self-immolation, organizing withdrawals from the CCP and accusing the Chinese government of selling organs of imprisoned Falungongers) means to interrupt the business of the Chinese government. Although the group has not created any problems for the government in recent years, the possibility of it pulling another "stunt" inside China is always a concern for the Chinese government.

May is indeed all "red"

Nationalistic Chinese see "red" in May, not the "red" of the unity of proletariat of the world (International Labor Day falls on May 1) but the blood of Chinese being killed during the accidental bombing by a U.S. B-1 of the Chinese Embassy in Belgrade on May 8th ten years ago. Although the Clintons are very popular in China (Chinese like Hillary Clinton even more after her refusal during her recent audiences with Chinese top leaders to openly criticize China for its questionable ways of treating its own citizens), and President Barack Obama has inspired the Chinese about what democracy can achieve, if domestic instability looms large in China, the government may play the card of nationalism and demonize the United States. If this is the case, May 8th might be a sensitive date. The recent confrontation between the USS Impeccable and five Chinese "fishing" ships in the South China Sea certainly is contributing to the possibility of serious U.S.-China friction that may test the new Obama Administration and top Chinese leaders. The question is whether China and the U.S. can be good stakeholders, if not exactly partners, in dealing with global recession and other thorny matters.

But May has another important anniversary, namely, the 90th anniversary of the May 4th Movement. May 4th has a special place in Chinese people's collective memory, a double-edged sword that can be used by different groups of people to serve divergent purposes. To those Chinese who are demanding political liberalization, May 4th is a symbol of rejecting China's corrupt government, defying authorities and forcing China to adopt an alternative development model. In the eyes of those Chinese who declare that no Western-style democracy suits China, as was emphasized on March 10th by Wu Bangguo, chairman of the Standing Committee of the National People's Congress, May 4th represents the epitome of China's frustration over the hypocrisy of Western liberal democracy. After all, the entire movement was triggered by President Woodrow Wilson, who allowed

Japan to take over China's Jiaodong Peninsula. The perceived sellout by President Wilson, who championed national self-determination, caused severe disillusionment among a small group of Chinese intellectuals. They rejected Western liberal democracy and accepted the Soviet model as the solution to China's crisis. They formed the CCP in 1921, which rose to power 28 years later. Both sides can play the anniversary in accordance with their political needs. It is extremely important for the government to seize the initiative.

June 4th is a day of "infamy"

Exactly a month after May 4th, there is the sensitive 20th anniversary of the June 4th crackdown in and around Tiananmen Square, a day of infamy for the Chinese democracy movement. The incident actually began on April 15, 1989, when Chinese students began to mourn the passing of Hu Yaobang, who had been dismissed from the position of general secretary of the CCP due to his liberal ideas, and ended on June 4th when tanks rolled into Beijing. A popular movement that called for democratization and an end to corruption was abruptly crushed. It was and is still being labeled as a riot aimed at overthrowing the CCP and the government. Every June 4th since 1989 Tiananmen Square has been put under special watch and nothing has really happened. Entering into the 20th year, there are renewed calls for the Chinese government to form a truth commission to confront the brutal acts of the government. Parents who lost their children during the incident have even begun to hold meetings in order to seek compensation and apologies. It is hard to imagine anything can happen on this particular day given the heightened alert of the government. Nevertheless, it is a day that the people's government would like to wish away, a memory it would like to see evaporate.

October 1 is the golden birthday of the republic

The next big anniversary is October 1. Sixty years ago, Mao Zedong stood on top of Tiananmen and declared that the Chinese people had finally stood up. It is a day that was born out of blood and tears, a day that came after millions were killed during the civil war from 1945 through 1949, a day on which all Chinese are constantly reminded to be grateful for the CCP and to feel proud. This year, the proud Chinese people may feel even prouder when President Hu Jintao reviews a military parade at Tiananmen Square. Mao did it, followed by Deng Xiaoping and Jiang Zemin respectively. However, for the first time, there are questions regarding the necessity of such a civil-education event. Is it wise to do so when the economy is floundering? Is it worth spending so much for such a spectacle when funds can be better spent on improving the social security network and healthcare coverage for the farmers? Will People's Liberation Army veterans, yet another group of people who feel angry about unfair treatment after serving the nation, be included in the parade? What about migrant farmers? Could they be included in the parade in addition to showing off the PLA's war-making/nation-defending equipment?

General Fang Fenghui, Grand Marshall of the parade, told deputies of the NPC recently that all efforts will be made to save funds in preparing and organizing the parade. After all, will ordinary citizens of the republic be allowed to walk around the Square and observe the parade on the National Day? If they are, they will certainly be awe-struck and proud. But will they continue to believe that because they were liberated by the CCP, they must always and forever believe that the Party will always serve the people and secure a government of them, by them and for them? Since no one can guarantee such an answer, this day is, alas, also deemed sensitive.

2009 is not 2008

For all Chinese, 2008 was initially meaningful for only one thing: China hosting the Summer Olympic Games, an event seen as a coming-out party for China. In the months leading up to the big event, there was a snow storm in January that saw hundreds of thousands of migrant workers stranded in train stations in Southern China and power lines out of operation for weeks. There were violent protests against the presence of ethnic Han Chinese in Tibet and other areas inhabited by Tibetans. There were interruptions of the Olympic torch relay in foreign capitals, including London, Paris and San Francisco. And there was the May earthquake that claimed 90,000 lives. The Chinese government managed to overcome all these interruptions and successfully host the Summer Olympic Games. Many Chinese scholars claim that the unprecedented efforts of disaster relief through national mobilization in the wake of the earthquake in Sichuan, and the best ever Summer Olympic Games, have shown the world not only that China has entered the club of powerful nations but that its development model can also be applied to all other developing countries. Arguably, hosting the Olympic Games has rallied the Chinese nation. The absence of such a rallying cause and the worsening of the economy may make it harder for the Chinese government to sail through the year without major interruptions.

The country is big and the Party has to be strong

It is more than a little ironic that a government whose leaders are ideologically focused on whole-hearted service to the people would have no trust in the people and actually fear things could careen out of control in a year that should be dedicated to celebration and post-Olympic Game relaxation. It is sad to think there are other things that may make 2010 and 2011 sensitive so that activities of the media, NGOs and conferences would need to be restricted. Shanghai will host the

World Expo in 2010, and 2011 is the centennial of the overthrow of the Manchu dynasty and the beginning of the republican era in China.

China has changed in the past 30 years since the beginning of opening up and reform, but one thing has yet to change: the government seems to be always possessed by fear: fear of possible social chaos, of losing the mandate of heaven, and of the possibility that the legitimacy of the CCP will be questioned by ungrateful citizens. Wu Bangguo, the number-two man of the nine-person CCP Politburo, declared on March 10th that without the CCP controlling everything, "a nation as large as China will be torn by strife and incapable of accomplishing anything." The Party has to be strong, and any effort that is designed to weaken the Party is criminal and has to be relentlessly crushed.

The herd of ox is unpredictable

While government fear is constant, the people are no longer the same: they are no longer a herd of ox, quiet, obedient, blindly loyal and aimlessly hardworking. The majority of them is upset but silent. A small like-minded group of them likes to complain and is becoming keener on questioning the legitimacy of the Party. With social and economic conditions deteriorating, this small group may be able to mobilize the silent majority. Anniversaries and other small events could become the trigger for massive protests.

We will see how 2009, the year of the ox, is to be lived by the Chinese people and their leaders. Is it going to be a year of national pride or a year of lost hope for more change? We are waiting for the final verdict.

Yawei Liu is Director of The China Program at The Carter Center, Atlanta, Georgia.

Taiwan Strait Security Challenges

Albert Willner
Vol. 8 No. 2
Spring 2009

The recent thaw in relations between mainland China and Taiwan shows encouraging signs of producing results. Efforts by China's President Hu Jintao to reach out across the Strait, Taiwan's presidential election last year of Ma Ying-jiou and increasing economic ties have further improved communications and set the stage for even greater cooperation. Responses by the United States and neighboring countries to improvements in cross-Strait relations and political change in Taiwan have generally been positive. Yet underlying these developments are pressures and suspicions that could exacerbate rather than relax tensions.

To be sure, the transition in Taiwan from the nationalistic Democratic Progressive Party's Chen Shui-bian to the Kuomintang's Ma by itself meant that the cross-Strait environment was bound to improve. After eight years of relatively continuous verbal challenges on the diplomatic, political, military, and information fronts, both sides were well positioned to take advantage of change brought about by the election of a new government in Taiwan. Following Ma's inauguration in May 2008, both sides have moved quickly to take advantage of new opportunities. The U.S. and others also breathed a sigh of relief that the 2008 election results would set the stage for the easing of tensions.

Beijing and Taipei quickly agreed to address issues of importance to domestic and international audiences. Starting in July 2008, direct flights between China and Taiwan increased threefold, reducing costs and travel time for business people and tourists. Direct sea transport has expanded, as has mail service, allowing for increased economic and cultural exchange opportunities. Interest in developing mechanisms for food-safety oversight and resolving problems has gained traction to address, in part, concerns about "tainted goods from mainland China."

The two governments are looking to broaden exchanges in other areas as well. Beijing is allowing students, professional actors and state journalists to attend school, perform on stage, and work for extended periods in Taiwan. Top Chinese bureaucratic officials, including some military officers, have been given greater latitude to visit Taiwan, although, to date, official visits by Chinese defense officials have been limited. An unprecedented call by President Hu for China-Taiwan military-to-military talks may also create new opportunities for engagement, although Ma has said serious military talks are not a priority at this point.

Both sides have sought to reinforce existing venues and foster new dialogue to advance the relationship. Beijing's leadership recently restated its commitment to using the Cross-Strait Economic, Trade and Cultural Forum by holding talks with Taiwan representatives in Shanghai in December 2008. The Forum's three areas are receiving the most attention in part because they are generally supported and less controversial among domestic constituencies and offer the best chance of early and visible success. Both governments can rightly cite the increased exchanges and dialogue for enabling greater cross-Strait economic and cultural gains in these areas and helping to assuage concerns about the potential for conflict.

Indeed, China has also indicated that Beijing would be amenable to working with Taipei to expand the latter's international space. In late April 2009, Ma announced that Beijing would not object to Taiwan's participation as an observer in the World Health Organization, and specifically in its governing World Health Assembly. Taiwan has agreed to use the name "Chinese Taipei" at these meetings and, while additional details continue to be worked out, this action indicates another positive step in the relationship. Underlying these advances, however, fundamental challenges remain.

Despite these advances, the growing Chinese military buildup in the air, at sea and on land coupled with Beijing's refusal to renounce the use of force against Taiwan has the potential to detract from gains being made in other areas. China's development of combat aircraft carrying missiles with a greater range than any Taiwan equivalent, its expanded submarine program, announced interest in developing an aircraft carrier, and ever-increasing number of improved missiles opposite Taiwan all continue to raise serious concerns and heighten the threat to peace in the region. Regular training missions by Chinese fighters, ships and submarines in and around the Taiwan Strait add to insecurity and increase the chance of an accident or a miscalculation. The lack of transparency accompanying this buildup, highlighted yet again in the most recent U.S. Defense Department China Military Power Report, further raises concerns in Taiwan and elsewhere not only about Chinese capabilities but about how Beijing expects to use its emerging military power. China's 2009 White Paper on Defense, designed to address transparency concerns and released on U.S. President Barack Obama's inauguration day, was widely viewed as insufficient in its efforts to address questions about either Chinese capability or intent.

The military growth and lack of transparency do little to calm concerns of the United States and China's neighboring states. The potential for accidents and confrontation in the air and at sea remains high not only in the Taiwan Strait but elsewhere, as debate over China's offshore zones and disputed islands remains unresolved. This was recently demonstrated again in March 2009 during a series of incidents in international waters in the South China Sea, when five Chinese ships and a Y-12 surveillance aircraft sought repeatedly to intimidate the USS Umpeccable, a U.S. research vessel by challenging it and trying to interfere with its freedom of movement. (China claims a 200-nautical-mile Exclusive Economic Zone, 188 miles beyond the internationally accepted 12-mile sovereign offshore limit.) These incidents, coming just two weeks after the reopening of U.S.-China military-to-military talks, highlight the willingness of Beijing to take risks in order to make claims in favor of its perceived economic space and challenge others on the high seas. This may be in part because the Chinese leadership feels the current international political, financial and diplomatic environment is favorable to taking such actions and that they will elicit little reaction. China's continuing disputes with Taiwan, Vietnam, the Philippines, Brunei, and Japan over various islands in the East and South China Seas increase the possibility of a crisis in the region, always with potentially far-reaching implications.

Across the Strait in Taiwan, in addition to the external threat, President Ma faces internal defense challenges as well. The Taiwan government recently released its first-ever Quadrennial Defense Review (QDR) highlighting the increasing international clout of mainland China at the expense of Taiwan, the need for Taipei to convert to an asymmetric doctrine to counter Beijing, and the desire for greater defense transformation and organizational innovation of its own forces. The document also states that while security tensions in the Taiwan Strait are gradually diminishing, mainland China continues to aggressively develop military weapons and systems and is conducting a three-front war on the legal, media and psychological fronts, placing continuous pressure on Taiwan's interests. Taipei's stated defense priorities remain focused on war prevention and transformation.

Ma's plan to advance a proposal initiated by his predecessor to convert to an all-volunteer force during the next five years brings with it the need to make some hard choices about how best to recruit and retain this new force, as Taiwan has relied on draftees to do much of its soldiering over the past sixty years. At the same time, there remains much discussion within Taiwan as to how best to meet the China challenge. In late 2008, a debate arose between the Taiwan National Security Council and senior leaders in the Ministry of Defense about whether to focus more on an Army-centric, hard-shell defense of the island, or whether to continue developing a joint air-naval-ground defense plan that had received extensive attention during the previous decade. The outcome of this debate has significant strategic implications for how Taiwan intends to defend itself, particularly in a place where time and space are extremely limited. Part of this debate centers on how best to make use of constrained resources, maintain public support for the military, and properly adapt its defense while at the same time reaching out across the Strait. These issues are significant not only as Ma looks to rethink Taiwan's strategic plan but also as the executive branch deals with challenges from a legislative body balancing competing priorities. The deliberation process and increased accountability demanded of Taiwan's defense officials also reduce the chances that budget and strategic direction issues will be quickly resolved.

Recent news of a pay-for-promotion military scandal, independent-prosecutor investigations of Taiwan defense contractors, military accidents, charges of Taiwan Navy personnel involvement in the murder of a prostitute, and the attempted suicide of Taiwan's former top Marine have all affected morale and diverted attention of senior officials from the government's defense initiatives. As the Defense Ministry leadership works to respond to these investigations, Taiwan's ability to focus on QDR priorities and readiness could be negatively impacted. As serious discussions increase across the Strait, the need to have a strong and unified voice emanating from Taipei is exceedingly important. In a crisis, such a unified voice would be critical.

How best to resolve core sovereignty issues will remain the major challenge in the Taiwan Strait. Whether the relationship continues to improve or lurches toward crisis will depend heavily on what mechanisms are developed, accepted and implemented to address real areas of difference. China's concerns about continued U.S. arms sales and support for Taiwan's defense needs and Beijing's willingness to push back to solidify its own sovereignty claims bring potential risks to peace in the region. Taiwan's external and internal challenges in addressing broad defense requirements, and Ma's own need to walk a political tightrope by reaching out to mainland China without appearing to sell out Taiwan's interests, offer additional opportunities but also potentially raise risks and increase strain.

The role that the United States, Japan, the Republic of Korea, Singapore, Australia, the Philippines and others in the region choose to play, especially as states adapt to the current global economic realities, will no doubt have an important impact on the outcome. These countries, through bilateral and multilateral exchanges and organizations, are working toward improved defense cooperation – as shown by actively pursuing military talks, disaster relief, search-and-rescue training, and broader exercise programs aimed at meeting common interests and challenges. Timely signals and exchanges among the regional actors that address communication, and in particular how best to deal with a crisis, will be important in allowing the work of improving cross-Strait ties to continue. Mainland China and Taiwan are clearly seeking to advance common interests critical to maintaining peace and prosperity in the region. As Beijing and Taipei move forward, keeping the peace in the Taiwan Strait and surrounding areas will require careful attention and a renewed commitment by all involved.

In the end, significant questions remain which could dramatically affect process and outcome. For Beijing, if the end-goal remains unification, what is the best way forward? President Hu and the senior leadership may be willing to work with Taipei and to assuage international concerns by taking a slow and measured approach to fully resolving differences, including possibly even an interim peace agreement. Would this approach be acceptable to those in China who are interested only in Taipei's capitulation, possibly along a much faster timeline? What kind of additional pressure does this place on a Communist Party already deeply concerned about maintaining its legitimacy in China? In Taipei, what are President Ma's own short- and long-term goals, and will he be able to make a supportable case within his own party and the broader Taiwan electorate? Will the Taipei leadership be able to craft a plan that addresses complex Chinese, American and neighboring states' interests and concerns? Will change in the status quo create its own momentum in fueling even greater expectations, or will it cause greater resistance to such moves? Fundamental change across the Strait clearly starts with realistic goals being set in Beijing and Taipei in line with their strategic interests. Achieving preferable outcomes will most likely, however, require managing expectations and interests well beyond the immediate control of both capitals.

Albert Willner is is the Director of the China Security Affairs Group, CNA China Studies, in Alexandria, VA.

Obama Gets Good Reviews in China

Mary Lewis Grow and Rebecca Dong
Vol. 8 No. 2
Spring 2009

Views in China about America's new president range from the superficial ("He's so handsome!") to the thoughtful ("He's extremely smart but we worry that his policies may not help China"). While there is no unanimity in the reasons Chinese give for approving of the Americans' choice in the 2008 election, there does seem to be an almost uniform lack of criticism of Barack Obama here that extends, often, to outright enthusiasm.

During the spring, 2009, several young women, graduate students at the University of International Business and Economics in Beijing, spoke effusively when the subject of Barack Obama was introduced. One, Yao Li, said, "He seems confident and competent to lead the U.S., and the reason is that he smiles a lot." Another, Sarula, said, "He is a peace-lover. [During the campaign] he said [that] if elected president, he would withdraw the majority of the armed forces [in Iraq] as soon as possible. It would be different from the policy of the Bush administration. He is making efforts to [have] his people live in a comfortable, peaceful environment."

Their friend, Liu Xin, liked the fact that Obama had succeeded on his own merit. "U.S. presidents [often] come from a rich family, like Kennedy and George W. Bush," she said. "Often, they get help from their families when they begin their political careers. When they participate in a presidential campaign, their families support them, not only with money but also influence. I learned that Obama was born into a very ordinary family. His father divorced his mother when Obama was very young. Obama once lived a very difficult life. It can be said that he started from scratch...He strived to succeed bit by bit. In 2008, he participated in the presidential campaign [ran for president]. Depending on his wonderful speeches and his smile, he succeeded at last. During his whole career, he could not get any support from his family. All that he could depend on was himself. He started from the grassroots but ended as president. His story is a good example of the American Dream."

Yao Yao referenced her friend's view in her own reply:

"I think he is a very attractive man, with distinctive qualities. During the presidential campaign, he made a lot of amazing promises to the American people. We are looking forward to seeing how he will keep his promises in such a complicated and difficult international situation. The financial crisis is striking the whole world and Iraq is still not peaceful.

"My friend said that what Obama achieved depended on his own ability. I agree that he achieved a lot without [the benefit of] a prominent family background. We admire him for this. In China if you want to be successful, you must rely on relationships and networks. However, Obama cannot do without the support of the Democratic Party and his colleagues. You know, that's politics!"

A young man handing out flyers for his travel agency at the gate of the same university said that he thinks "Obama is very humorous." When asked if he thought that Obama would be good for the relationship between China and the United States, the young man hesitated, uncertain about whether Obama would act in China's interests. When asked why he harbored such fears, he said that he thought most leaders did what was best for their own country, and Obama would not be unique if he looked to U.S. interests first.

A Muslim restaurant owner in his forties gave verbal applause to Obama's stance on Guantanamo. Obama, he believes, is likely to release most detainees. He also expressed pleasure at Obama's conciliatory outreach to the Muslim world.

A shopkeeper in Dashenze, the cutting-edge arts neighborhood in the northeastern part of Beijing, smiled when asked for her views about the new American president: "He's very strong," she said, "and he will have to be if he is to help lead the United States out of its current crises."

A wide sampling of Beijing cab drivers offered a range of quick impressions: "Obama bi Bush hao." ("Obama is better than Bush.") Why? "Because he doesn't/ didn't like the war in Iraq." Although "da Bush" (George Herbert Walker Bush) is always compared favorably with his son, "xiao Bush," at least one cab driver said that even "da Bush" liked war [the first Gulf War] too much. Several drivers gave a two-word answer: "Ting hao," "Very good," but were unable to say why they liked the new American president, some adding that they didn't really know enough yet about Obama to have an informed opinion.

One young Beijing cabbie was surprised to learn that Bush was no longer president, and, in fact, had left office three months earlier!

In Shanghai, a cab driver twisted around in his seat to be sure that his American passenger had understood his very positive opinion of Barack Obama. "I like him very much," he said, with strong emphasis. "He has a good heart."

Opinion in Shanxi Province differed little from that in the capital, even though opportunities for conversation with foreigners and exposure to the western press in Shanxi are extremely rare. The faces of a retired middle-school principal and his wife lit up when asked about America's new president. They were very happy when Obama was elected, they said. A young teacher of English and friend of the retired couple concurred, though none of the three could give issue-based reasons for their favorable impressions.

A rare criticism of Obama was expressed by a salesman in a small store in Pingyao, an old city in Shanxi famed for its well-preserved walls and watch towers and its former status during the Ming and Qing dynasties as the banking center of China. "He's too smooth by half," he replied when asked if he had an opinion of America's new president. Although unable to elaborate on this impression, and in spite of his store's prominent display of the iconic Shepherd Fairey portrait of Obama on a large package of matches (on sale in dubious company with other match boxes whose covers featured Hitler, Stalin, Che Guevara, and Mao), the young man's negative view was far from tentative.

Andrew Kaiser, a young American who has lived and worked for twelve years in Taiyuan, the provincial capital of Shanxi Province, reported seeing an off-the-beaten-track shop named "Obama" even though its wares had no apparent connection to the new U.S. president. The naming of the store was, in Kaiser's view, most likely a marketing decision determined by Obama's widespread popularity.

Of three representatives of the Chinese media who offered their impressions of President Obama, two spoke very approvingly of him, but one echoed the reservations of the shopkeeper in Pingyao. Tao Libao, a former employee of CCTV, now in his thirties and running his own TV production company, said, "When Obama talks in everyday life, he still talks as [if] making a speech to the public. I [feel] he might not know or be willing to expose his true feelings. So I feel he's not sincere, or he doesn't know what to do with the topic he's talking about."

The slightly older vice-president of a Shanghai media group offered a much more positive take on the new U.S. president. Obama's energy, he believes, will kindle a corresponding energy in his compatriots, particularly among younger and middle-aged Americans. Younger people are more likely to be open to the kind of change that Obama represents and more willing to take a chance on going in new directions, said the Shanghai media executive. He expressed optimism about Obama's relationship with China and said that most Chinese are ready and willing to see him as a friend.

Forty-two-year-old film producer and former university professor Wang Guangli spoke of the youth, vigor, and confidence he sees in Obama, and he wishes the new president success. If Obama is not successful in addressing the huge problems that face the United States, Wang Guangli will not see his failure as a lack of competence but rather as a reflection of the enormous problems he is dealing with. And, he said, many of the Americans' difficulties are world issues as well.

Wang Guangli draws on his film and media background to assess Obama's star power, which he believes Obama to have in abundance—more than many movie stars. While Obama's charisma may cause some people to judge him as superficial, notes Wang Guangli, it may give him a greater platform for success. So far, he says, Obama has not disappointed expectations. Other charismatic presidents have turned out to be successful, he adds, citing Ronald Reagan and John F. Kennedy, among others.

Obama's youth may be one of his biggest assets, according to the film-maker. Young people are willing to learn, he says. They are flexible in dealing with conflict, and young leadership is capable of dealing with old problems in new ways.

With access to many media sources, Wang Guangli has had frequent opportunities to observe Obama on television. In fact, he notes, he has taken for his own use one of Obama's most popular slogans: "Yes, we can!"

He Xiangmin, an economist and university administrator currently serving as Vice President and Executive Director of the China Association for International Education, spoke thoughtfully about Obama and American politics. Chinese believe, he said, that Democrats are better for their country during hard economic times, but they worry because Democrats often are more confrontational with China over issues of human rights and protectionism. Traditionally, he said, it usually takes two to three years for a new Democratic administration to adjust its relationship with China. But he is hopeful that Obama's learning curve will be shorter since, unlike Bush, who tried to tell the rest of the world what [the U.S. thought] they should be doing, Obama seems more inclined to work collaboratively and listen to others. He believes that Obama is less likely to use war as an instrument of foreign policy and thinks there is greater world-wide trust that he would use war only as a last resort.

He Xiangmin is relieved that Obama seems to have softened his protectionist stance, which makes China more amenable to helping the U.S. with its trade imbalance issues. China's agreement to use some of its excess foreign reserves to purchase $10 billion worth of American goods will work to both China's and the U.S.'s benefit, since it helps reduce China's dollar reserves and will help stimulate the U.S. economy. Even though the recent agreement works to the benefit of both countries, He Xiangmin believes that it also is a reflection of trust and goodwill towards Barack Obama and recognition of his desire to work well with

China.

"While Bush said, in effect, 'Do as we say, not as we do,' Obama shows greater respect for other people and other cultures," says He.

China knows, says He Xiangmin, that unless the U.S. recovers, there will be no global economic recovery, so its policies will reflect a desire for the economies of both countries to be strong. But, he added, China wants – and should have – a bigger voice in World Bank and IMF policy formation.

Another Chinese economist, a prominent and influential policy advisor, Zhang Jianye (not his real name) made different points when talking about Obama and his administration's relationship with China. Contrary to many of his friends who said that the United States would never elect a black man as president, this economist predicted Obama's win, saying that he believed that the United States had already changed enough to break the racial barrier in its electoral politics. And he knew, he said, that Americans very much wanted a change from the Bush years.

In general, he said, Chinese have a very favorable impression of Obama, in spite of their gratitude to George W. Bush for honoring his commitment to come to the Beijing Olympics [and, although he didn't mention it, GWB benefited from the affectionate memories Chinese have of the first President Bush, who served as first U.S. envoy to China, though unofficially, after the breakthrough in U.S.-China relations].

Much like his fellow-economist, He Xiangmin, Mr. Zhang noted that new American administrations often start out by picking a fight with China. That Obama did not start off this way has pleased China, the South China Sea incident notwithstanding. He spoke admiringly of the restraint demonstrated by both sides during and after that incident and said that Obama's sending Secretary of State Clinton to China so early in his administration was a positive sign.

Mr. Zhang believes that the make-or-break issues between the U.S. and China will be economic, not military. He acknowledged China's complicity in amassing so much U.S. debt, saying that just as an individual should not continue lending to a friend who is already deeply in debt, China contributed to the problem by continuing to lend to the U.S. long after it should have been apparent that the U.S. was spending far more than it was saving and would have trouble repaying its loans.

He expressed particular concern about the issue of whether the U.S. repays China in inflated dollars or amounts that equal, in real value, the amount of China's loans. He believes that the U.S. is morally obligated to guarantee that its repayments will not erode the real value of China's foreign exchange reserves.

"Don't create China as an enemy," he counsels. China does not have a history of territorial expansionism, he argues, even in the past when its naval fleet dwarfed those of any other country in the world. And China does not want to see the hegemony of the dollar changed, though they may not like it. But they do not propose to change it.

As Obama goes forward, Mr. Zhang observed, he may need seasoned and experienced economic hands such as Lawrence Summers and Timothy Geithner, but he also should reach out to more new people who perhaps have not been as deeply enmeshed in the financial structures and institutions that have failed so badly.

It is important for both China and the U.S. that our new president succeed. Although Obama's foreign policy is still unfolding, Mr. Zhang believes that he has made a good beginning in reaching out to other countries.

Ending on a note of hope, he added, "Americans are adaptable and learn from their mistakes."

Mary Lewis Grow has been visiting China for extended stays since 1990. She runs a non-profit in Northfield, MN. Rebecca Dong has worked with media companies in China since 2002, including National Geographic, and is based in Beijing.

Challenge and Change in Chinese Export Controls and Industry Compliance

Gary K. Bertsch
Vol. 7 No. 2
Spring 2008

Questions have been raised over the years about the will and ability of China's governmental and industry actors to comply with national and multilateral trade regulations. More than ever before, Beijing has been responding to those questions, particularly in recent months and years. High-ranking officials have vowed and – more importantly – taken actions to strengthen China's export control system and industry compliance.

At the same time, the effectiveness of the Chinese government and industry efforts and the extent of progress are difficult to judge in the short term. The threat of illicit exports is always there. Even developed countries like the United States – countries that take nonproliferation seriously and have had considerable experience with export controls – are regularly embarrassed by violations on their soil. Controlling illicit trade everywhere – including China and the United States – remains a work in progress.

So although we can expect violations of export controls in China and elsewhere, what we are looking for is progress in law, commitment, compliance, enforcement and prosecution. My research and experience in China suggests that considerable progress is being made.

China's Progress

The development of Chinese export controls under market socialism began in the mid-1990s. This resulted from the continuing opening and reform of the Chinese economy. If China was to participate in high-tech and defense-related trade, and take on international responsibilities to match its economic ambitions, it was becoming clearer to officials that they would have to become more involved in international export control and compliance. They would also want to develop their own national export control system.

China promulgated formal export control regulations in 1995. More specific regulations followed regularly in subsequent years. Nuclear trade-related export control regulations were instituted in 1997 and 1998. The Chinese government issued its first set of arms export control regulations in 1997. In 2002, China promulgated a series of new or amended regulations covering a host of strategic commodities and technologies, including chemical, biological, missile and munitions. These regulations included controls that were reflective of the multilateral export control arrangements, such as the Nuclear Suppliers Group. Further, in 2004, the National People's Congress passed an amended Foreign Trade Law that undergirded China's domestic system of export controls and included a wider range of criminal and administrative penalties for violations than had existed previously.

These initial steps were promising, but questions remained about the political will and commitment required to implement the new regulations. While implementation challenges continue, indications are that the Chinese government has worked conscientiously to implement its national control system in this decade. It has also sought to integrate China into multilateral export control regimes. China has now joined the Nuclear Suppliers Group and begun membership talks with the multilateral Missile Technology Control Regime, the Australia Group and the Wassenaar Arrangement.

During this decade, China has issued regular white papers on nonproliferation emphasizing the importance of export controls. It is my distinct impression that they are committed to seeing their ideas turned into practice. Clearly, high level officials have made the strategic choice to be among the advanced industrial countries working to integrate the needs of both trade and security. The Chinese obviously want to continue to promote international commerce. They also realize that in order to do so, they must become more vigilant in controlling commerce that could jeopardize national and international security.

To balance and pursue these trade and security interests, the Chinese government began a series of outreach and training exercises for its Customs service and major strategic enterprises. It has instituted an electronic export licensing system. It is also now demanding that internal export control compliance systems be implemented in its export-oriented enterprises.

Among the regulatory developments, the Ministry of Commerce (MOFCOM) issued Circular No. 548 in December 2005 on Reform of the Administrative Approval System for the Import and Export of Sensitive Items and Technologies. This circular commissioned China's provincial and municipal governments and other local entities to serve as the initial reviewers of export permit applications for dual-use goods and technologies. By year's end MOFCOM and GAC (General Customs Administration) issued the most comprehensive regulation to date, Order No. 29 on Measures for the Administration of Import and Export Licenses for Dual-Use Items and Technologies. These measures created a comprehensive national control list, expanded the scope of "catch-all" and transit/transshipment controls, and laid the foundation for broader coverage of technology transfers. These and other developments have convinced me that Chinese authorities are serious about export control and about trying to integrate the concepts of trade and security.

The Chinese government took specific actions to strengthen Chinese export controls during this period. In July 2006, Notice No. 50 applied dual-use export licensing and clearance procedures to a list of graphite-related items with potential nuclear application. MOFCOM also released an updated Dual-use Biological Agents and Related Equipment and Technologies Export Control List that subjected new bio-related items to control. These new Chinese bio-related regulations reflected growing international concerns about the threat of bio-terrorism and developments within the related multilateral export control arrangement— the Australia Group. This provided further evidence that China was striving to be more in line with international standards and arrangements.

In August 2006, Chinese authorities established requirements related to specific civil aviation parts with potential missile dual-use application. In September 2006 they issued new regulations on the import and export of precursor chemicals. In December they promulgated and amended regulations on the control of nuclear exports, aligning themselves more closely with the multilateral Nuclear Suppliers Group. On the last day of 2006, the GAC and MOFCOM issued the latest version of China's control list. In 2007, China continued its regulatory enhancement efforts by amending and strengthening its controls on nuclear dual-use items and technologies, and issued another update to its national dual-use control list.

To complement its regulatory efforts, China has expanded its industry outreach initiatives. Numerous workshops, seminars and conferences have been organized and implemented in various industry sectors throughout many regions of the country. This training and outreach is increasingly offered in China's provinces and localities, not just in major centers like Beijing and Shanghai. Increasing information about export controls, in both Chinese and English, is being made available on Chinese government agency websites. Public information and industry awareness is critical to regulatory compliance. Chinese officials are now making significant efforts to keep relevant industries and exporters informed. To lay a foundation for the promotion of industry compliance, the Chinese Ministry of Commerce issued guidance on the development of internal export control programs for Chinese industry in August 2007.

Despite the increase in industry export control outreach, numerous Chinese companies have been sanctioned in this decade by the United States government for not abiding by U.S. law and international norms relating to trade and security. While these sanctions relate to a diverse and complicated set of cases and issues, their imposition was not entirely surprising. Among other things, it is clear that the Chinese search for markets and trade has been aggressive. The growing level of commerce pushed the limits in various areas and was bound to run afoul of U.S. hopes and expectations in various areas. What will be of significance is what was and is being done by firms that were sanctioned.

Let me describe my personal observations concerning one of these companies– China North Industries Corporation. NORINCO is the import/export marketing company under one of China's top state-owned defense holding companies, China North Industries Group Corporation (CNGC). Research and manufacturing companies under CNGC produce both civilian and military items, including arms, machinery, optical-electronic products, oil field equipment, chemicals, and light industrial products. CNGC operates over 150 large- and medium-sized companies employing approximately 800,000 people.

In the early part of this decade, the NORINCO division of CNGC was the subject of several government sanctions. The first sanctions were imposed in 2003 for exports that "could assist the Iranian missile program." Few details were provided by U.S. authorities, but they did raise the company's behavior as evidence that the Chinese export control system was still deficient. Beginning in 2004 and 2005, NORINCO officials decided to begin developing an internal compliance program. NORINCO's corporate leadership has issued a clear and unmistakable commitment to building a responsible corporate export control program. Both the corporate leadership and mid-level officials have worked diligently to set up an effective internal compliance program to inform and educate their workforce about the program and the need for export controls.

NORINCO has made a great deal of progress. No new sanctions have been imposed upon NORINCO in recent years. The NORINCO experience is being closely watched, and followed, by other Chinese firms. Key enterprises among China's nuclear, aerospace, aviation and electronics industries have taken note. It is my impression that an increasing number of large Chinese enterprises are recognizing that informed corporate officials, responsible export behavior, and an effective internal compliance program will be good for business. Rather than limiting exports, responsible export controls in line with international standards can be "trade enabling." Companies that have a responsible corporate culture and internal export control compliance program will be more likely to avoid sanctions and be competitive in more markets.

Yet much work remains to be done in China. Some of China's exporters are slow to recognize the need for compliance and the opportunities before them. Some feel that internal compliance programs are an unnecessary cost and unacceptable distraction and burden. Some believe that they can avoid the responsibilities and that the growing focus on industry compliance will blow over. Many of China's smaller and medium-sized companies remain in dire need of export control information, training and help in raising awareness to develop internal compliance programs. In addition, there are still deficiencies in the overall Chinese export control system. The current system remains without comprehensive controls on brokering activities, intangible technology transfers, and conventional dual-use items and technologies. China is not fully integrated into the Missile Technology, Australia Group, and Wassenaar multilateral export control arrangements.

Clearly, Chinese compliance with national and international trade regulations remains a work in progress. However, my experience demonstrates that significant progress is being made in the area of export controls. This progress should not be ignored. It is real, and should be recognized and lauded. It will have many benefits for China, the United States and the world. Among other things, export control development and compliance build an environment allowing expanded trade and technological relations. Here in the United States, we often complain about the China-U.S. trade imbalance. If China develops effective export controls, the U.S. government will likely recognize this and develop greater confidence in Chinese trade behavior. This may lead to a relaxation in U.S. controls on high technology exports to China. For example, if U.S. authorities have confidence that U.S. high-tech exports will remain with recognized and responsible end-users, and will not be diverted to military-related uses or to other states, the present U.S restrictions are more likely to be relaxed. At a minimum, Chinese and U.S. authorities should continue to build on the areas of common interest in the nonproliferation area and the expanding strategic economic dialogue to explore avenues of increased cooperation in export control and compliance.

The opening, reform and development of the Chinese economy over the last thirty years is one of the most significant events on the world stage. Chinese willingness and ability to comply with evolving national and international regulations and norms will be one of the major factors affecting China's overall success over the next 30 years. My study and experience have convinced me that the benefits of trade compliance in a global economy are significant. Some are already being realized in the U.S.-China commercial and other bilateral and multilateral trade relationships. Continued Chinese development in, and commitment to, nonproliferation, export controls and industry compliance will bring more benefits.

China, the United States and the global community can increasingly find themselves in win-win situations. Continued progress in this field will support peace, prosperity and security in the 21st century.

Gary Bertsch is Professor Emeritus and Founding Director of the Center for International Trade and Security at the University of Georgia, Athens, Georgia.

The Road Ahead:
A Preliminary Assessment of the 17th Congress of the
Chinese Communist Party

Yawei Liu

Vol. 6 No. 3
Fall 2007

Enough time has passed since the 17th Party Congress of the Chinese Communist Party was held in March, 2007, to begin the assessment of a political event that the Chinese president referred to as being characterized by Party unity, policy victory and theoretical achievement of the Sinification of Marxism.

Three of the many benchmarks are crucial to understanding the effects of the 17th Party Congress. First, will the CCP be able to break away from the past practice of using the Congress to lionize the incumbent or soon-to-retire top leader as a genius whose ideas will be designated as the beacon of the Party's orientation? Second, will there be a smoother and more institutionalized power transfer? Will Hu Jintao attempt to handpick his successor, much like he was selected by Deng Xiaoping, or will the Party's institutions play the role of king maker? Third, and perhaps most crucial, will long-awaited political reform be planned and launched in the next five years? We will examine these questions in order.

On the issue of Congress lionizing out-going leaders, the signs are not positive. President Hu Jintao is being lauded in official discourse for championing a "harmonious" society. In this, Hu is merely following a long Communist tradition of thinking that only a small group of leaders are best informed, wisest, and most qualified to represent all the people and make the best possible decisions for them. Karl Marx had figured out all solutions to the problems of his day. V.I. Lenin founded the first Communist nation by "scientifically" modifying Marxism. Mao Zedong adapted Marxism and Leninism and turned China into the people's nation. Deng Xiaoping salvaged China from the brink of an economic and social collapse. Jiang Zemin made China prosperous. Hu's brilliance and genius is on the lips of all Party leaders. He is given credit for China's economic, cultural, scientific and social achievements. Why has Hu failed to eliminate the bad practice of self-glorification? Either he desires it or it is forced upon him. If we are a little cynical, we can even say it is Chinese to be ruled by a "divine" leader. But surely making an individual's ideas synonymous with the Party Charter is feudalistic, vain and out of step with the principle of popular sovereignty. This is a new source of disillusionment with the top leadership of China.

Signals are mixed on the question of transferring power. Even though before the closing of the meeting there were rumors that Xi Jinping, former governor of Fujian and Party secretary of Zhejiang, would be promoted to the Standing Committee of the Politburo, it was a surprise when it happened. Observers inside and outside China believed that Li Keqiang would emerge as heir apparent. The thought was that Hu would do what Mao and Deng had done before: select a successor long before he exited from center stage. This did not happen, and Xi "helicoptered" to the position that was supposed to be Li's.

There are multiple explanations for Xi's sudden elevation. It could be a result of his experience and qualifications:

He is a "princeling" and therefore someone who could be trusted with the paramount power of the Party. After all, this power did not come easily. It was obtained as a result of the blood and sweat of the generation that included Xi's father.

Xi was sent down to the countryside as a youth for seven years in Northern Shaanxi and presumably understands rural issues better than anybody else.

He worked in Fujian for numerous years and has acquired deep knowledge about Taiwan.

He served as Party secretary in Zhejiang, one of the engines of China's economic growth and a province where state ownership of enterprises is almost obsolete.

But other political factors could be at the heart of the decision. Perhaps the Party is becoming factionalized, and Xi is the compromise candidate for the top job five years from now. Or it might be that there is real intra-Party democracy, and Xi's takeoff is an outcome of popular support among senior Party leaders in China.

We will have to wait for Xi or other insiders to tell us the real story later. The very fact that the conventional candidate (whose performance is questionable and whose charisma is unknown) was moved to the second position is a good sign. While people in the U.S. lament partisan politics and lack of political unanimity, for the Chinese political system to liberalize, dissent, disagreement and dissonance will be key. They are needed to weaken the power monopoly and make personnel and policy decisions more contentious and therefore more democratic. The Party needs more democratic discussion and less centralism. Decision by majority vote is the only effective way to root out tyranny by a few.

On the issue of political reform the picture is even more complex. Perhaps Hu Jintao understands a people's democracy is not possible without intra-Party democracy. As reported by Xinhua, Hu is against arbitrary decision-making in the Party. He declares that all possible efforts should be made to increase transparency in Party affairs and to "oppose and prevent arbitrary decision making by an individual or a minority of people."

On enhancing intra-Party democracy, Hu calls on all Party members and organizations at all levels to "take the lead in upholding the authority of the Constitution and the law." He also says that the Party will strictly implement democratic centralism, and improve the system that combines collective leadership with division of responsibilities among individuals. Local Party committees will adopt a voting system to decide on major issues and to appoint cadres to important positions.

Hu asks the Party to experiment with the standing committee system, arguing that the Political Bureau of the Central Committee should regularly report its work to the plenary session of the Central Committee and accept its oversight, and that the standing committees of local Party committees at all levels do likewise at plenary sessions of local Party committees.

The Party is supposed to reform the intra-Party electoral system and improve the system for nominating candidates and electoral methods at the grassroots level (namely the township and town party committees). Of crucial importance is the fact that Hu has endorsed the experiments of the so-called "two ballot" electoral system promoted by Sichuan and other provinces in the past few years. In this system, candidates for Party committees are supposed to be determined by a popular poll and a vote by all Party members. Hu vows to gradually extend this system of "direct" election of leading members of Party committees, and explore various ways to expand intra-Party democracy at the local level.

This long overdue democracy roadmap seems intriguing and does contain actionable plans. However, one needs to assess its weight and priority in the context of the overall political report and the undercurrents of the internal debate on political reform. If one checks how Hu Jintao stresses socialism with Chinese characteristics, pessimism and confusion kick in.

What is socialism with Chinese characteristics? According to Hu Jintao, it means the localization of Marxism. "We will, under the leadership of the CCP and in light of China's basic conditions, take economic development as the central task, adhere to the Four Cardinal Principles and persevere in reform and opening up, release and develop the productive forces, consolidate and improve the socialist system, develop the socialist market economy, socialist democracy, an advanced socialist culture and a harmonious socialist society, and make China a prosperous, strong, democratic, culturally advanced and harmonious modern socialist country."

Hu also says in his report, "Practices since the publication of the Communist Manifesto nearly 160 years ago have proved that only when Marxism is integrated with the conditions of a specific country, advances in step with the times and is tied to the destiny of the people can it demonstrate its strong vitality, creativity and appeal. In contemporary China, to stay true to Marxism means to adhere to the system of theories of socialism with Chinese characteristics."

Mao Zedong localized Marxist theory by mobilizing peasants to catapult the Party into the cities. Deng Xiaoping localized Marxist theory by saying that improving people's lives supersedes revolutionary fervor. Jiang Zemin localized Marxist theory by defining what the Chinese Communist Party represents. Hu Jintao is in the middle of a new theoretic localization. We know Hu's new "scientific outlook" implies balancing economic development, reducing the galloping gap between the rich and the poor, and maintaining social justice. We hope that an element Hu outlined in his speech will be promoted by the Party: building a harmonious society that not only guarantees social justice, but also political liberty and equality. In other words, China should be built into a nation in which people are respected as the sole source of legitimacy and ruling mandate.

Such a policy would not be a brilliant localization of classic Marxist theory of class struggle, alienation, capital, surplus value, and imperialism. If this is not a betrayal of classic Marxism, it is at least an Edward Bernstein type of revisionism that the Chinese Communist Party once spent lots of resources and passion to condemn.

Even if Hu desires to push political reform, the structure of the Party could stand as a major obstacle. On paper, implementation is simple. General Secretary Hu Jintao issues marching orders and the 31 provincial and municipal Party secretaries, representing the will and wishes of 73.4 million Party members, carry out the plan. The problem is that many of the Team of 31 will very conveniently forget what they have seriously said and solemnly pledged and go astray. (Chen Liangyu, who used to be a powerful member of the Team of 31, is currently waiting for a verdict and possibly wondering what he has done wrong to fall from the top all the way to the bottom.) Their unprincipled and sometimes shameless deviation will be mimicked on a massive scale by those who are below them.

The more this kind of straying happens, the more often ordinary citizens question the Party's truthfulness and sincerity. Anger builds up. How to vent popular anger so that it does not escalate into a quintessential Marxist moment of revolution like the Paris Commune in 1871 could become a central concern.

Problems could easily arise elsewhere as well. Any sudden political, social or economic crisis (such as Taiwan becoming bolder in pursuing independence, global economic recession causing the Chinese economy to tank, the U.S. making China a hostile nation, popular discontent in China caused by inflation, environmental degradation, lack of healthcare coverage) may catch the Party by surprise. Harmony and legitimacy are interconnected. If legitimacy is questioned and even challenged, harmony will be as thin as rice paper. In the Internet age, China may not have the luxury of waiting until the next Party Congress five years hence to settle on a new policy direction and glorify a new leader and new principles. The only way for the Party to ensure unity, solidarity and popular support is to introduce a viable system through which people's opinions can be freely expressed and people's input can be meaningfully incorporated into how Party and government leaders at all levels are chosen.

Yawei Liu is Director of The China Program at The Carter Center, Atlanta, Georgia.

Domestic Politics

Can Development Dissolve Spears and Shields? Hu's 'Harmonious Socialist Society' betwixt Mao Thought and Deng Theory

Stephen Herschler
Vol. 6 No. 2
Spring 2007

October's meeting of the 6th plenum of the 16th Central Committee of the Communist Party of China (CPC) concluded by passing "The Resolution on Some Issues in Building a Harmonious Socialist Society." This document presents not only the Party's current goals for China's development, but it also introduces Hu Jintao's original contribution to Marxist ideology. Yet certain aspects of the Resolution's wording are striking, specifically the prominent role it gives to 'contradictions' in contemporary China. Hu Jintao is generally considered to have been selected by Deng Xiaoping to succeed Jiang Zemin. 'Contradiction,' however, is very much the brainchild of Mao Zedong. Yet Deng could only pursue 'reform and opening' after superseding Mao Thought with his own. This raises the question: how can Deng's political progeny utilize a core Maoist concept without subverting his political benefactor's reform agenda?

The position of generational Party leader includes providing ideological leadership. Hence, the history of CPC leadership is not just one of leaders but, more important, of their ideologies: Mao Zedong Thought, Deng Xiaoping Theory, Jiang Zemin's 'Three Represents,' and now Hu Jintao's 'Harmonious Socialist Society.' Each leader's ideology combines his own novel formulations with particular elements strategically selected from previous leaders' guiding thoughts, thereby suggesting overarching ideological continuity between leaders as well as their own particular program's being the logical consequence of that which had preceded it. These ideological frameworks generate the Party's 'line' and 'guiding thought' for national policy in a particular era. As China is governed by the CPC, all these guiding thoughts necessarily adhere to some general Marxist conception of historical development. That is, they understand history as a linear process of development (or a path), traveling through sequential world historical stages, leading eventually to one ultimate destination: Communism. Thus, each leader's ideology necessarily addresses two issues: where China currently is on the path and how China can best progress along the path. To better understand the challenge and opportunity Hu faces in melding elements of Mao Thought and Deng Theory with his own specific program to develop China, it helps to first review his predecessors' distinctive conceptualizations of what generates progress.

Mao: Progress through 'Contradictions'

Uniting elements from Daoist philosophy with a Marxist dialectical view of history, Mao emphasized that 'contradictions' not only constituted all things in the natural world as well as in society, it also was the generative force for development in all domains. A country's progress was driven by contradictions between social groups, more specifically through class struggle. Mao's 'Sinicized' Marxism helps to explain some of the distinctive features of Chinese political-economy under his rule. In terms of economics, the Great Leap Forward can be understood as reflecting Mao's belief that the contradiction between a society's desire for development and its poor economic base could be resolved by society unleashing a revolutionary effort to advance agriculture and industry. Of course, the Great Leap Forward proved to be one giant step back for China's economic development. In terms of politics, the Great Proletarian Cultural Revolution was rooted in Mao's determining that not only had contradictions persisted after the Chinese Revolution but that these contradictions included antagonistic contradictions between groups upholding the Revolution and those opposing it. 'Grasp class struggle as the key link' was proclaimed to be the national priority, spawning a series of campaigns against prominent national Party leaders. Of those officials who survived being the target of such campaigns, many were restored to full power only after Mao's death in 1976. One of them was Deng Xiaoping.

Deng: Progress through 'Development'

Upon Mao's death, Party elders who had recently suffered the vicissitudes of Maoist politics, with Deng Xiaoping as their de facto leader, moved quickly to revise the Party's guiding thought. 'Grasp class struggle as the key link' was replaced by 'economic construction as the focal point.' Party leaders affirmed that with the Communist Revolution, China had entered into a new phase of history. Mao's works applied mainly to an era of 'war and revolution,' a time in which class struggle was indeed the primary contradiction in society. After the Revolution, however, China had entered into an era of 'peace and development.' Accordingly, the main task facing the Party and the people, the core contradiction, had changed from 'Liberating the productive forces' to 'Developing the productive forces.' Mao's glory lay in leading the 'first' political revolution, while Deng Xiaoping's glory lay in spearheading China's 'second revolution,' economic development.

If 'contradiction' was the lynchpin of Mao's political-economy, for Deng it was 'development.' Deng coined the mantra of his era when he stated, "Only development is firm reason," while undertaking his 1992 tour of Special Economic Zones. Deng's words launched a national campaign to resume market reforms stalled in reaction to the political and social upheaval in the spring of 1989, a campaign that culminated in the CPC's embracing of market economics in the 1993 "Party Resolution on Some Problems in Constructing a Socialist Market Economy." Deng's tour and its reformulation into Party guiding thought ignited in China a development frenzy which has yet to abate.

Deng's focus on development informed both his conceptualization of China's current historical stage as well as the means by which China could best progress on the path. While the international environment was a phase of 'peace and development,' China itself was in the 'primary stage of socialism'—a very long phase indeed, one lasting perhaps 100 years. The goal for this phase was economic development. Deng's understanding of what actually spurred development is connoted by a fundamental re-conceptualization of stages that occurred under his tenure. Dengist views of international political-economy measure a country's position and its progress primarily according to certain development indicators, most importantly economic statistics. This view of development parses the countries of the world into three stages of development: advanced, developing and 'falling back.' These categories are relational, meaning that to categorize a country as 'developing' is to implicitly evoke the existence of other countries further ahead or behind on the path. Characterizing China as a 'developing' country clearly indicated China to be further behind on the path relative to other countries. As history is linear, China's progression would require that it cover some of the same terrain as the world's economic forerunners, the advanced industrial nations. Accordingly, Deng called for learning from more 'advanced' countries and adopting (with 'appropriate revisions') their advanced economic and management techniques. He warned that to not develop meant to 'fall back,' relatively speaking, which posed the risk of China once again being 'beaten and humiliated' by other, more developed countries.

Deng also differed from Mao in how he conceptualized the domestic impetus for development. First, China needed to 'open to the outside world,' that is, engage with international markets. Second, China's development was to be spurred by local development. Accordingly, the reform era involved an incremental devolution of decision-making and fiscal autonomy to local entities. While Deng did say that China's relatively 'advanced' localities could and should 'pull along' the country's poorer regions, he emphasized that in China's current stage of development nothing should be done that might dampen the vitality and rapid development of China's local economic vanguard, including such measures as imposing high taxes or undertaking excessive redistribution of wealth.

Hu: Progress Through "Development 'Dissolving' Contradictions"

Contradiction, essential for understanding Mao Thought, is all but irrelevant for understanding Deng Theory. Thus, it is striking to read in the October 2006 Resolution, "No society can be without contradiction; society always develops and progresses through the movement of contradictions." The Resolution concurrently affirms, "For society to be harmonious, first it must develop." In other words, the Resolution gives weight to both Maoist and Dengist conceptions of development.

Closer examination of contradiction's deployment in the Resolution, however, reveals that its framing is very much Dengist, with China's place on the path, the characteristics of the international environment, and China's location relative to other countries following formulations crafted during the Deng years. Building a 'harmonious socialist society' is presented as a natural consequence of the Party's success in upholding 'reform and opening' as well as 'modernization construction.' Peace, development, and cooperation remain the major trends of this historical stage but China's development also occurs in a context in which peaceful development is challenged by a number of factors, including an ever-intensifying competition between countries' comprehensive strengths. While reform has helped China develop significantly, the Resolution underscores that China "will continue to face pressure due to advanced countries' continued superiority in economics, technology and other areas for some time to come." In other words, China remains 'backward' relative to more advanced countries. Thus, economic development remains vital for China's progress, perhaps for its very survival, and China will continue to learn from more advanced countries.

Only after a meticulous framing of China's stage of development does the Resolution finally introduce the concept of contradiction, using a formulation that comes directly from Dengist views: "the primary contradiction in our country's society remains the contradiction between the people's material & cultural needs and society's backward production." In other words, the central contradiction is between economics and society. This basic contradiction spawns a series of more specific contradictions which become the focus of the Resolution. They include: the legal system, economic disparities, the employment system, morality and culture, creativity and innovation, public administration, and environmental issues. The breadth of topics covered results from the Resolution's function, namely, to set forth a guiding thought pertinent for almost every organizational component of the country's immense governing apparatus.

The way in which these different components are analyzed suggests a divergence from the Dengist development model. The Resolution's structure connotes that these constitute contradictions naturally produced by China's current stage of development; indeed, they are necessary products of China's previous development successes. While Deng had emphasized local initiative and experimentation, the Resolution's wording indicates that the central government will become more involved in cultivating and regulating social and economic development within the country. This notion of governance comes forth in how contradictions are conceptualized in the Resolution. China's current contradictions are not constituted by struggle. Rather, they are amenable to hua-jie, a word that evokes dissolving and clearing up. It is clear that the central government is to play a decisive role in dispelling contradictions through a range of national policy endeavors, including: transfers of fiscal receipts, educational reform, work on a social security system, societal and governmental morality campaigns, legal and administrative institutional reforms, etc. Indeed, within the body of the text, the word 'contradictions' all but vanishes, indicating that the focus is less on contradictions than on national governmental measures to dissipate them.

Can Development Dissolve "Swords and Shields"?

To briefly position Hu's notion of development relative to Mao Thought and Deng Theory, Hu shares with Mao an understanding of contradiction as being an unavoidable phenomenon in a country's development. However, he uses the term to describe potentially harmful social phenomena that naturally arise in the course of a country's development. That is, unlike Mao, he suggests contradictions are the unfortunate product of development rather than as development's generative force. He sides with Deng in affirming that China's primary contradiction is between society and economics, and hence economic development remains China's primary goal. Development's primacy over contradictions is affirmed by development's not only producing contradictions but also resolving – or rather, dissolving – them. He differs somewhat from Deng, however, in granting the central government a greater leadership role in comprehensively managing and directing development. Indeed, one is tempted to conclude that Hu's China is taking a more socialist path.

The "Resolution on Some Issues in Building a Harmonious Socialist Society" sets forth Hu's plans for China's future through 2020 – a date that is likely to be well into his successor's term. The Resolution has already had an impact on

Party and public discussions of social reform, as evinced in numerous articles assiduously analyzing contradictions in essentially every social and economic domain and proposing means of 'dissolving' them. As all the current members of the standing committee are engineers by training, it comes as little surprise that they conceptualize Chinese society as a complex mechanism that Party policy can make run more smoothly, particularly if the policy adheres to a 'scientific development view.' While Hu's coining of a 'Harmonious Socialist Society' seeks to define the national agenda for the next decade, he may have less control over how contradictions are used. Chinese renders the term by combining the character for spear with the character for shield, objects not easily dissolved. The Party has its work cut out for it in this stage of Chinese development, both in managing China's current contradictions and in managing how people conceptualize and apply 'contradiction' to Chinese society.

Stephen Herschler is Provost and Associate Professor of Politics at Oglethorpe University, Atlanta, Georgia.

Domestic Politics

The New Politics of Equity

Baogang Guo
Vol. 6 No. 2
Spring 2007

China's political development is undergoing an important transformation. Beijing's latest emphasis on the need to address social and economic concerns of the average person has led to a series of new policy initiatives. These initiatives are designed to more fairly distribute wealth and promote the quality of human development. The politics of equity-maximization have returned to the center stage of politics, though not in its radical form.

Economists such as Arthur M. Okun have observed the phenomenon of the efficiency-equity tradeoff.[1] According to this hypothesis, efforts to improve efficiency can degrade equity, and excessive welfare distribution will lower growth rates and reduce economic efficiency. On the one hand, extreme egalitarianism leads to incentive traps, free-riding, high operating costs, and corruption, and on the other, extreme inequality leads to social unrest, erosion of social cohesion, and instability.[2]

China's success with reform has greatly improved China's economic performance since 1979. However, the widening income gap between rural and urban populations, the emergence of the new urban poor, the worsening regional disparity between the more developed coastal regions and the western part of China, and the widespread public criticisms of market-oriented reforms in health and education in recent years have put the reformers on the defensive. The mounting

---

1 Arthur M. Okun, *Equity and Efficiency: the Big Tradeoff* (Washington D.C.: The Brookings Institution, 1975).

2 Giovanni Andrea Cornia and Julius Court, *Inequality, Growth and Poverty in the Era of Liberalization and Globalization*, policy brief no. 4., World Institute for Development Economic Institute, the United Nations University.

pressure for social justice has resulted in escalating numbers of disputes, complaints, and protests. Can technocratic managers survive the onslaught of the moralists who demand that the government provide fair and equitable distribution of wealth?

Many problems facing China today, such as inequality, immorality, insecurity, alienation, rootlessness, and ruthlessness can be linked to the relentless pursuit of efficiency and the neglect of human problems by leaders whose training is limited to science and engineering. Although technocracy, which has taken root in China's economic and political system since the 1980s, is an important step toward acquiring what Max Weber has termed a rational-legal basis of political legitimacy, the lack of popular sovereignty and the innate tendency toward oligarchic rule will eventually weaken the legitimacy of bureaucratic technocracy. Can China move beyond technocracy? Will China improve political and social equity without sacrificing economic efficiency? Can an optimal balance between efficiency and equity be achieved through proper implementation of an equity-maximizing policy?

The sixteenth CCP Party Congress, held in November 2002, and the tenth National People's Congress, held in March 2003, completed the power transfer from the so-called third generation to the fourth. This group of new leaders seems to have reached a consensus that reform has reached a critical point at which some policy adjustments must be made. They have proposed a new development model that may produce "a harmonious society" internally and "a harmonious world" internationally. They believe that this new model should be based not only on continued economic growth but also on fair distribution of the growth, unlike the unrestrained and unbalanced growth of the Deng–Jiang era. The upcoming Seventeenth Party Congress to be held fall 2007 will certainly codify this new developmental strategy and consolidate the policy changes initiated in the last few years.

Consider rural development. The government has taken steps to alleviate income disparity between rural and urban residents. The agriculture tax was abolished last year; a new rural health care insurance system has been expanded rapidly with heavy government subsidies; tuition and fees for all children attending rural schools have been waived; and a rural welfare program will be put in place to help peasants who live in poverty. All of these popular moves have large appeal to the rural population, and have enhanced the utilitarian dimension of the political legitimacy of the state.

Equity maximization has returned. Nevertheless, the new leaders neither intend to return to radical redistributive schemes nor to a bottom-up style of populism. Many Western observers have noticed the latest wave of new policy initiatives, and they consider it to be a Chinese version of the "New Deal." Notably, Hu

Jintao, the General Secretary of the Chinese Communist Party, has returned to ancient Chinese top-down populism. He has used the words "min ben," or "putting the people first," repeatedly in his speeches, and has proposed his "three peoples" principles. Premier Wen Jiabao shares similar views. According to him, from "Confucius to Dr. Sun Yat-sen, the traditional Chinese culture presents many precious ideas and qualities, which are essentially populist and democratic."[3] Both Hu and Wen want the government to respond to average people by addressing their social and economic concerns.

Is this an end to pragmatist ideology? Has China entered an era of enlightened elitist rule? Or is this just a new ideology designed to paper over problems and allow a continued emphasis on the Deng-Jiang policies of rapid growth? Is a new breakthrough in the making? It is apparent that the top-down style of populism is proactive and led by an existing elite group within the establishment. It differs from the bottom-up populism advocated by revolutionary modernizers because it does not appeal to the people directly, and it certainly has no intention of mobilizing the public to stand up against the establishment; instead, it calls for changes within the system. Its rise, therefore, should be interpreted as the government's preemptive response to an emerging governing crisis. The question is whether the people who run China mean it.

Baogang Guo is Associate Professor of political science at Dalton State College, Dalton, Georgia.

---

3 Wen Jiabao, *"Turning Yours Eyes to China,"* remarks made at Harvard University, December 10, 2003, transcripts from Harvard Gazette, December 11, 2003.

Assessing China's Villager Self-government: Are Elections Leading to Democracy?

Yawei Liu
Vol. 6 No. 1
Winter 2007

In 1988, China began allowing villagers to elect their leaders in an experiment that democracy advocates hoped would eventually lead to more pluralism throughout the political system. Today, the Communist Party is still in firm command of the high ground and villages are still holding elections. So, what has the experiment accomplished?

This article will offer an assessment, first looking at the various discourses on villager self-government and trying to determine if there is a consensus on the significance of this undertaking. It will then examine how this political act is transforming the political language, culture and landscape in China and aim to decide if villager self-government indeed constitutes an opening crucial for China's long overdue political reform. Third, it will address the questions: What is democracy? What is democracy with Chinese characteristics? And will the current village democracy lead to a fundamental transformation? – from a government of choice but little accountability at the lowest rung, to one of choice and accountability at each and every level, secured by institutions rather than by moral coercion and ideological purification. The article will then take a brief look at what the grass-root Party officials are saying and what Chinese peasants are doing in the era of relative freedom and self-management.

While it is hard to separate the past, present and future of a development that is so young, this article will focus more on the period from November 1998 when the Organic Law was amended, to September 2005, when Premier Wen Jiabao repeated Peng Zhen's famous remarks to visiting foreign dignitaries: when villagers learned how to manage the village affairs they would then try to manage the township affairs.

When the National People's Congress was debating the Organic Law, Peng Zhen, chairman of its Standing Committee, remarked that introducing villager self-government was in line with the Chinese Communist Party's goal of making common people the masters of their own affairs. It was a very effective way to conduct a democracy seminar for the peasants. When they learned how to govern their own affairs, they would then try to learn how to manage the township and county affairs. In 1989, there was a coordinated effort to discredit the Organic Law and label it as a sinister plot derived from Western ideas of democratization. Peng Zhen and his supporters withstood the assault, stuck firm to the need for rule of law and said that a way must be found to allow peasants to hold local officials accountable. With almost a decade of persistent effort by the officials of the civil affairs apparatus, the Organic Law was finally amended and officially adopted. Another eight years have passed. What is the current discourse on villager self-government?

There seems to be little change among the top leadership of the Chinese Communist Party (CCP) in their view of the nature of villager self-government although there is a detectable shift of emphasis and priority. Jiang Zeming called villager self-government one of the three crucial reforms in China's countryside, as important as the beginning of the household responsibility system and the launch of village and town enterprises. In the political reports of both the 15th and 16th CCP National Congresses, Jiang identified villager self-government as the point of breakthrough for China's political reform. Since the ushering in of the Hu-Wen New Deal in late 2002, growing attention has been given to the solution of economic woes of the peasants and social instability in the countryside. From the campaign to promote open administration of village affairs to the elimination of taxes and fees, to the emphasis on increasing the income of the peasants, to the call to build a new socialist countryside, we see a pattern of devaluing rural democracy and accelerating pragmatic measures to create better conditions for peasants' access to education, healthcare and wealth.

This shift of emphasis at the top is indicative of which arguments among the watchers of villager self-government have found more responsive ears among the national leaders. Like the current divergent assessments of reform and opening up, the views of villager self-government are also sharply divisive. There are those who perceive villager self-government as a miracle prescription to the chronic diseases of the Chinese countryside and the stepping stone to the eventual modernization and democratization of China. For those who are less friendly to villager self-government, they see the alarming reemergence of the clans, the susceptibility by the broad masses of peasants to small materialistic incentives and indirect anti-government appeals, and the interruption of the development of village enterprises.

Those who are opposed to the expansion of village self-government have been aided by two factors: 1) the lack of linkage between the institution of village democracy and the growth of village wealth (and the misery among tens of millions of Chinese peasants who increasingly sense that they are actually victims of the economic reform that has made China such an integral part of the world economy), and 2) the CCP's concern that popular choice and strict accountability could undermine the Party's legitimacy, and its insistence on being the paramount decision-maker on all aspects of rural life.

This dichotomy between perceptions of villager self-government has existed since the debate on what to do with the peasants in the wake of the abolition of the communes in the early 1980s. The discussion of whether villager self-government is empowering the rural residents or emasculating the Party's leadership and whether it will make peasants feel happier or create obstacles for economic development, will continue in the foreseeable future and have a significant impact on the sustainability of villager self-government.

The renewal of the direct election of local people's congress deputies in 1978, and particularly the introduction of direct election of village committees in 1988, has led to a new sense of political ownership and a new awareness of what constitutes political legitimacy. Real competition at the village level – in places where local officials believed that the most cost-effective way of providing "guidance" was direct nomination of candidates, and direct election of village committee members from among multiple candidates – has led the residents to overcome initial suspicion of whether their votes would make a difference and to begin playing the political game more seriously.

The political scientists who study this new rural political development began to paint a very rosy picture of this undertaking and have even hatched a new field of study. They call villager self-government a "silent revolution" that will lead to the destruction of old feudalistic heritage and the birth of new civic virtues and political activism. They feel villager self-government is the beginning of a new wave of the encirclement of the urban centers by the vast countryside. Further, they wonder whether if the least-informed and -educated group are given the right to directly elect those who make decisions affecting them, then perhaps the better-prepared residents in the cities should be offered at least the same opportunity.

The echoes of the Chinese scholars have not only reverberated in the capitals and classrooms of European countries and the United States, but also have been heard by the top leaders inside the Forbidden City. This new language has not only crept into the speeches of the China-watchers in the West, but also has been melded into the political jargon of Chinese leaders. While the image-makers of China have achieved the goal of using villager self-government to prove the nascent rise of political reform in China, the praise of it by the top Chinese leaders in 1998 at the 15th CCP National Congress led to the unprecedented experiment of a direct election of a township magistrate in Buyun, Sichuan.

If we measure villager self-government using Robert Dahl's two attributes of democracy (contestation or compilation, and participation or inclusion), it seems we may call it a curtailed democracy in a restricted geographical area, always subject to outside forces it has no capacity to resist. Village self-government also seems to possess the features of both internal and external efficacy. If, however we used other criteria to determine whether villager self-government is democracy, with other universally recognized and accepted components, the answer becomes less certain and even doubtful.

In the context of Chinese political systems, both past and present, villager self-government can be described as meaningful democracy with Chinese characteristics, or, at least, as an embryonic form of a unique democratic practice that is different from other forms of democracy. First, it calls citizens' attention to the serious problem of the Chinese political system, i.e. the justice of the systemic design and the injustice of procedures. This injustice is caused by the woeful lack of executable procedures in choice and accountability matters and the gross manipulation of those procedures that have been laid out.

Second, villager self-government is operating within the context of a Chinese system whose center of gravity is located with the Party. The fact that a significant number of Party officials feel the cost of governance is so much lower when the right to choose their immediate leaders is given to the peasants may lead to a reorientation of the belief that the Party always knows best. In fact, practice of villager self-government has already trickled upwards and led to many trials of choice and accountability at higher levels.

Thirdly, direct village elections, with their competitiveness and their real impact on political legitimacy, governance and the initiatives of those who run and get elected by the ordinary voter,s are a reminder to those who are contemplating political reform in China that real reform does not have to be wholesale adoption of the Western system of multiple political parties and parliamentary supremacy. The Chinese system on paper is sufficient if the Party superstructure does not interfere with direct elections of township and county people's congress deputies and indirect elections of local officials such as township and county magistrates by the directly elected people's deputies.

Lastly, it appears villager self-government is conducive to solidifying the Party's legitimacy and likeability in the countryside. This may reduce the fear that is constantly on the lips of Chinese officials: that allowing the lowly common Chinese people to engage in democratic elections and decision-making at higher levels will lead to chaos and eventually break the back of the Party.

Yawei Liu is Director of the China Program at The Carter Center, Atlanta, Georgia.

A Novel Approach to Improving Rural Finance and Increasing Farmers' Income

Chuanhao Tian and Feijun Luo
Vol. 8 No. 3
Fall 2009

China's stunning economic growth since 1978 has resulted in a ten-fold increase in real GDP per capita, with an average annual growth rate of 8.6% in the past three decades (China Statistical Yearbook, 2008). However, urban incomes have continued to outstrip rural incomes – the per capita income ratio between urban and rural people widened to 3.3:1 in 2007 from 2.6:1 in 1978 (China Statistical Yearbook, 2008) – and the trend is a major concern for the government. A policy announced in 2004 to phase out agricultural taxes has not worked to reverse the income gap. Undoubtedly, this disappointing outcome calls for additional supporting measures for farmers.

Houses and lands (H&L) are the most important potential assets to farmers. Zhang and Liu (2007) estimated that the value of H&L accounted for approximately 74% of an average rural household's total asset value. However, current Chinese law prohibits the sale, exchange, transfer, or collateralization of rural H&L, which greatly impedes the growth of income to farmers. Ke (2007) found that in 2005 farmers' asset income only made up 2.7% of their total income. The prohibitions also constrain the development of rural finance since H&L cannot be used as collateral for loans. By June 2005, agriculture loans were just 5% of total loans issued by financial institutions (Hu, 2006).

Not only does the current law block the development of rural finance and the increase of farmers' income, but also it promotes even more inefficient use and unequal distribution of scarce land resources. All rural Chinese households can apply for free land sites from their villages and build houses on those sites, but the lack of a market mechanism makes for inefficient land use. From 1997 to 2005, 97 million rural people migrated to urban areas, but they still retained ownership of their rural H&L even if it became vacant. Numerous studies (e.g., Zhang & Lu, 2006; Han, 2008) show that vacant H&L and even vacant villages have become more and more common. In addition, the system fosters excessively large H&L holdings by some farmers and insufficient ones by others. Needless to say, vacant and excessively large H&L causes tremendous waste of land resources, something that should be corrected to foster sustainable economic growth.

Reforming the current land law can bring enormous benefits to farmers as well as society. Should farmers be allowed to sell H&L, migrants would be able to collect large sums of money by selling their vacant H&L and using the proceeds for consumption and savings, generating new sources of economic growth. Should farmers be allowed to exchange or transfer H&L, they would be able to trade old houses for new ones provided by real estate developers and receive monetary compensation, which could improve farmers' living conditions and attract capital to rural areas. Should the collateralization of H&L be allowed, farmers would be able to receive more agriculture loans and invest in profitable businesses, and that could lead to booming rural markets.

Some of this already is happening beneath the surface. Despite the official prohibition on the sale, exchange, transfer, or collateralization of rural H&L, underground markets have sprung up for rural H&L. In developed regions such as the Yangtze River Delta, the Pearl River Delta, and the vicinities of Beijing, rural H&L have entered the market through rents, transfer, partnerships, collateralization, and other means (Jiang & Liu, 2003; Wang 2003; Huang, 2006). However, the lack of guaranteed H&L ownership in underground markets serves as a drag on further investments and a disincentive to improving the quality of buildings.

To mitigate the serious problems in the current rural H&L law, some local governments have piloted gradual reforms under the acquiescence of the central government. Chengdu began issuing official certificates confirming property rights of farmers in 2008, providing a basis for the transfer and social utilization of H&L. Tianjin, Guangzhou, Fusan, and Jiaxing enacted a policy of exchanging rural H&L for city dwellings in the hopes of bestowing benefits on both the local governments and farmers. Zhejiang Province allowed for the transfer of H&L collateralization. Together, these policy experiments in different regions, although their impacts cannot yet be fully evaluated, provide valuable experience for future reforms in rural H&L law nationwide.

Land-law reform is not immune to risks, so it is vital to anticipate and control those potential problems. The risk that policy makers are most concerned with is the emergence of homeless farmers. For example, most farmers have no health insurance. If they become seriously ill, they might sell their H&L to pay for expensive medical services if they were able to do so. Therefore land law reform should not stand alone; rather, it needs to be coordinated with reforms in other areas such as health care. The recent health care reform, which aims to provide basic medical services to all farmers and make medical services affordable, is a beneficial foundation for land-law reform.

Another risk of land-law reform involves corruption. Policy makers need to safeguard against self-interested officials making decisions during the reform process that benefit themselves and other special-interest groups at the expense of farmers. If this is allowed to happen and becomes rampant, land-law reform could actually threaten social stability.

To conclude, there is a growing interest in reforming the current land law, which constrains rural finance and income growth for farmers. Land-law reform can benefit farmers, city dwellers, and government units, as evidenced by the experimental reforms in some regions. Every reform carries risks; however, the risks are manageable as long as governments prioritize people's interests and build in safeguards against self-interest and corruption. The recent health care and social security reforms in rural areas provide a good environment for the land-law reform.

Disclaimer

The findings and conclusions in this article are those of the authors and do not necessarily represent the official position of Zhejiang University or the U.S. Centers for Disease Control and Prevention.

References

Han, K. (2008). 启动中国农村宅基地的市场化改革. Starting the Market Reform of China's Rural Houses and Lands. 《国家行政学院学报》, 2008(4):4-7.

Hu, S. (2006). 工业反哺农业、城市支持农村的社会经济分析. Socioeconomic Analysis of Industry Subsidizing Agriculture and Cities Supporting Rural Areas. 《建设社会主义新农村理论研讨会暨中国农村社会学学术年会论文集》 2006.

Huang, X. (2006). 征地制度改革和集体建设用地流转之我见. Personal Views on the Land Procurement Reform and the Transfer of Collective Construction Lands. 《农村工作通讯》, 2006(11):40-41.

Jiang, X. & Liu, S. (2003). 土地资本化与农村工业化——广东省佛山市南海经济发展调查. Capitalization of Rural Lands and Industrialization of Rural Areas — Investigation of Economic Development of Guangdong Province, Fushan Nanhai. 《管理世界》, 2003(11): 87-97.

Ke, B. (2007). 加快推进现代农业建设的若干思考. Some Thoughts on Accelerating Modern Agriculture. 《农业经济导刊》, 2007(2):5-7.

National Bureau of Statistics of China. China Statistical Yearbook, 2008.

Wang, X. (2003). 全面保护农民的土地财产权益. Protect Farmers' Interest on Land Property Assets. 《中国农村经济》, 2003(10):9-16.

Xinhua News Agency. Farmers Benefit from Agriculture Tax Cut. March 6, 2004.

Zhang, D. & Liu, Q. (2007). 河南省武陟县农民贷款担保协会调查与分析. The Survey and Analysis by the Farmer Loan Guarantee Association of Henan Province, Wuzhi Village. 《农业经济问题》, 2007(5).

Zhang, Z. & Lu, X. (2006). 农村宅基地的整治与增值. The Regulation and Development of Rural Houses and Lands. 《调研世界》, 2006(1):19-22,26.

Chuanhao Tian is Associate Professor in the College of Public Administration at Zhejiang University, China. Feijun Luo is a health economist at the U.S. Centers for Disease Control and Prevention in Atlanta, Georgia.

Fiscal Incentives and
Local Government Behavior in China

Wanda Bailing Wang

Vol. 6 No. 1
Winter 2007

Local-central government relations are a hot issue in China today. Many problems result from fuzzy division of responsibilities and the difficulty of designing incentives to achieve multiple goals. These problems include local protectionism, trying to out-do each other in offering incentives to foreign investors, over-investment resulting in redundant construction, poor investment choices, and over-zealous growth.

In China "local government" refers to all types of sub-national governments. As a key part of the central-local dynamic, China's fiscal system plays an important role of macro-regulation, exerting great influence upon local governmental behavior by defining the scope of fiscal revenue and expenditure, and the responsibilities and rights of fiscal management between the central government and local governments. China's fiscal system has undergone a series of changes as part of the overall reform process in order to improve resource allocation and overall economic productivity. This article re-examines the previous narrow notion of a fiscal system as applied in China, analyzes the changes that have taken place, and offers suggestions for further reform.

The structure of China's fiscal system has shaped local governments into "quasi-market agents" that demonstrate great enthusiasm in participating in resource allocation activities. As a result, they have made great contributions to recent national economic growth. At the same time the present fiscal system also brings many negative influences to local government behavior, and thereby is hindering the economy's development of healthy growth in the future. The way China reforms its fiscal system from here will directly affect the behavior of local governments. It is critical that China deepen its fiscal system reform to optimize local governmental behavior to ensure economic development in the long run.

At present, the pivotal question for China's economists and officials is what kind of fiscal system can promise the greatest success in maintaining economic stability and lead to the establishment of a more equitable redistribution of income and efficient allocation of resources. There seems to be consensus that a strong government has some advantages with regard to the functions of stabilization, redistribution and provision of public goods and services. Meanwhile, with the move to a more market-oriented system, governments should work to become macroeconomic regulators instead of direct organizers of microeconomic activities.

Local government behavior under different reform systems
Early Reforms

After years of under a very top-down fiscal system where local governments did not have control over their budgets, reforms in the early 1980s experimented with various contractual systems between different levels of government. The contractual fiscal system was characterized by defining a fixed sum paid (or received, if subsidized) to the central government by a local government. This approach clarified the tasks assigned to local governments and the benefits they would receive, and provided greater incentives to encourage local growth. Within the term of the contracts, local governments could arrange their own revenue and expenditure according to their goals of regional economic and social development. However, their increased independence also dramatically changed their behavior.

First, because local budgets increased with local revenue, local governments had a strong motive to develop their regional economies and new opportunities for profit generation. However, since they did not have taxation power and because of shortages in local revenue in the face of the need to develop infrastructure, local governments began to depend more on revenue that could be raised and spent outside of the official budget. This included the unwarranted pooling of funds, as well as arbitrary charges and fines that helped cover the gap between expenditure and revenue. The unintended consequences of these efforts were that they undermined fiscal discipline and distorted the internal mechanism of the contractual system.

Second, in order to take advantage of resource allocation and system arrangements, local governments bargained hard with the central government to win decisions on system choice and policy-making that were slanted in their favor. Many different contracts resulted, with little consistency across local governments, and the short timeframe of each contract led to short-term-oriented behavior.

Third, because local governments had control over extra revenue generated above their negotiated contract with the central government, local governments tended to interfere with the management and other decisions of firms within their jurisdiction, frustrating enterprise market reforms.

Tax Reform in 1994

Compared to China's tax system prior to 1994, the Tax Sharing Reform, enacted in January 1994, instituted monumental change. The reform was aimed at (1) unifying and perfecting the tax system so that tax collection could be administered on the basis of law instead of on the basis of administrative discretion and bargaining; (2) simplifying the tax system; (3) assuring governmental revenue; (4) enabling reasonable sharing of tax revenue, and taxation authority between the central and local governments; (5) using taxation as an instrument to control the economy and adjust resource allocations; and (6) ensuring tax burden equity.

The 1994 Tax Reform divided tax revenue into three categories: central taxes, regional taxes, and central/regional government shared taxes. These divisions are close to those often used in countries with market-oriented economic systems. Administratively, two levels of tax administration were established: the state bureau of tax administration (responsible for central government tax and central/regional shared tax administration) and regional tax administration (responsible for regional/local tax only). The central and provincial tax administrations each levied its own taxes on the basis of the new tax laws. As a result, local governments could in theory enjoy more freedom over their own revenue, while helping to ensure the central government's revenue. At the same time, the changes that resulted in decentralized tax authority would give incentives to local governments to work towards good economic performance to increase the tax revenue generated.

The appeal of the revenue-sharing system embedded in the 1994 Tax Sharing Reforms is that it put a highly elastic central revenue system at the disposal of local governments. With this system, local governments were allowed to disburse expenditures if they generated more revenue. This created powerful fiscal incentives for local governments to promote local economic growth in order to raise revenue and create employment.

Alongside these positive incentives a number of serious negative results also emerged, largely due to the lack of institutional guarantees, making the balance of power between central and local governments difficult. The changes lead to resentment due to the absence of popular representation, which meant local officials were appointed by the central government according to their ability to promote economic growth rather than being elected locally. Therefore, when local officials did not live up to the expectations of their constituents, they did not suffer any serious consequences, and they easily avoided transparency in their negotiations with the central government.

Policy Options to optimize local government behavior

Local governments play a very important role in national economic development. Without optimal local government behavior, it is impossible for a society to achieve a healthy development in the long run. Broadly speaking, there are a lot of factors affecting the negative behavior of local government in China. However, from the above analysis, we can see the fiscal system is one of the most important. In this context, taking measures to further fiscal-system reform can not only optimize local government behavior, but can also bring long-term positive effects for future development. Several policy reforms are needed.

Ultimately, no matter what the central or the local governments do, their power comes from the society they serve. But the self-inflation of power by the government sometimes exceeds the scope given by society. With no adjustment mechanism, the result is often inflation of government bureaucracy and rent-seeking, where the government officials impose hefty fees on productive economic activity. After 20 years of reform in China, the growing social strength of the citizens makes it more urgent that local officials monitor their own behavior. To accomplish this, the reforms should support the development of three kinds of social organizations: (1) those organizations that can improve the degree of self-discipline of the agents in the micro-economy, such as trademark and intellectual property protection, accounting and audit expertise, asset assessment and stock exchange information and transactions; (2) those organizations that can improve the organization and smooth functioning of markets, such as judicial process and other organizations that support social service and social welfare; and (3) those organizations that can improve the coordination between macro-control and micro-activities, such as trade associations, labor unions and professional associations.

Under the present fiscal system, local governments are both players and referees. In order to improve their local performance, there is need to separate the evaluation of local government officials from a simple measure of rapid growth in output, which to date has driven local officials' promotion and their chances of winning favorable policies for the future. Freeing enterprises from government intervention in their operations and putting more resources in the hands of the populace would be more desirable. In the future, some of these types of measures must be taken to reshape local governments and turn them into lean and efficient governments by making clear their rights and responsibilities.

Wanda Bailing Wang is Professor and Vice Dean of the College of Management at Dalian Maritime University, Dalian, China.

China's Equity Markets:
Recent Reforms Encourage Domestic Investors

Yanping Shi and Penelope B. Prime

Vol.6 No.2
Spring 2007

On 27 February 2007, Chinese equity markets fell almost 9%. Hours later other global markets plunged far and fast, including those in Europe and the U.S. Such a link between China's equity markets and others was unprecedented. Analysis conducted in the aftermath confirmed that capital flows between China and other markets are highly controlled, and therefore were not the main cause of changing stock prices. Subsequent volatility in the Chinese markets has not spilled over to other markets. Nonetheless, global investors are now watching China's markets closely.

The purpose of this article is to provide background on the development of the Chinese equity markets in order to underscore the point that the recent volatility of China's stock values was a result of domestic capital and an array of domestic decisions.

Some Background

In the early years of reform in the first half of the 1980s, Chinese companies around the country began issuing shares as a way to raise money. The first formal rules for issuing corporate shares were formulated by the Shenzhen government in the mid 1980s. At the national level, the State Council established China's two exchanges, Shanghai and Shenzhen, in the early 1990s, but with mainly state companies initially being listed. Other regional over-the-counter markets and experimental exchanges were closed. The official purpose of the two exchanges was to promote a share-holding system in order to reorganize and improve the performance of state owned enterprises—in other words, this was not initiated as a process of privatization (Walter & Howie, 2003).

The share-holding system categorized shares by their relationship to the state, and only non-state shares could be traded. This particular structure has defined the character and development of the equity markets in China. By 2002, listed, non-tradable stock controlled by the state had decreased to two-thirds of total shares due to sales to the public. However, firms where the controlling share was owned by the state still comprised more than 80% of listed companies, and more than 40% of the firms had one large shareholder controlling 44% or more of the shares, which was almost always a state entity.

Market Development

Despite the heavy state presence in these markets, as part of the reform effort to create an environment where firms behave in profit-maximizing, cost-minimizing ways, China introduced rules aimed at creating better corporate governance. China passed a series of corporate laws that, among other things, required firms to have boards of directors with at least two independent members. As a result, by the end of 2002, 31% of the listed firms had some independent directors.

Another goal of the current stock-market reform is to convert non-tradable shares into tradable ones. Early on, both the authorities and academics in China began to recognize the disadvantages of having non-tradable shares (Zhang 2006). Attempts to fix this problem of equity division have been tried, but two observations can be made about those previous procedures.

First, political sensitivity lead to hesitation to take action that would harm state assets and public ownership at that time. Second, almost every reform arrangement before the latest one ignored the fact that tradable-share investors acquired equities of listed companies in a different way than the state. That is, investors in tradable securities based decisions on stock exchange rules and perceptions of the future value of shares, while the state acquired equity based on the planned economy regime.

As a result, tradable-share investors would vote by selling shares each time a reform with negative consequences for them was put in place. This naturally ended in big drops in the stock exchange index without mergers and acquisitions occurring because of the tradable and non-tradable regime. The biggest drop was about 50%, from about 2200 points in 2001 to 1000 points, in July 2005, in the Shanghai exchange after the last reform experiment. In that reform, referred to as "reducing the state share reform test," only 17 listed companies participated, accounting for less than 20% of the total, and the experiment lasted only four months. Despite the modest size of the experiment, the resulting market shakeout caused China's government to rethink how to reform the stock market.

In principle, in order to acquire the right to sell non-tradable shares, a holder (most were state entities and often were also major investors in the listed state-owned enterprises) should compensate the public shareholders in some way determined through bargaining. The reason is that initially when a state-owned company was listed, public investors paid a premium for its shares.

For example, suppose an accounting firm determined that company ABC had assets of 200 units where 100 represented equity and 100 represented debt. Then the 100 units of equity would be divided into 100 shares with face value of 1 Yuan per share, let's say, and then divided into three parts. The first 51% was issued to a state entity such as a government bureau; a second part (usually 29%) was issued to other state-owned enterprises at face value of 1 Yuan per share; and a third part, 30%, was sold to public investors at a premium price, say 3 Yuan per share on the date the company officially listed.

Due to this initial set-up, later arrangements were going to have to equalize the investment cost of non-tradable shares with tradable ones. In order to protect the public shareholders in this latest round of reforms and avoid either a moribund market or a big crash, the Chinese Securities Regulatory Commission designed a special voting system. Each compensation arrangement had to be passed by the voting system, and if not, the listed company needed to rearrange its compensation. In the end, the compensation arrangement varied company by company.

Examples of compensation schemes included transferring dividend shares to public investors, transferring dividend shares plus cash, transferring dividend shares plus options, etc.; however, the most common way was for the shareholders of the non-tradable shares to simply turn over some of their shares to those investors holding tradable shares. The public could sell those shares as soon as they were compensated if they chose, but the non-tradable shareholders were required to wait until they met other requirements. The most common requirement was that they had to wait one year after completing the compensation arrangement before they could sell any shares. In some cases the companies also promised additional compensation, such as not selling their shares unless the price reached a certain level, but these promises were not officially backed or required.

Largely due to the wide implementation of this reform, where investors who held tradable shares were appropriately compensated, starting in 2006 investors returned to the market. According to *The New York Times* (Yardley 2007), over two and a half million investment accounts were opened that year, and the Shanghai Composite Index increased 130 percent. On February 27, 2007, however, many investors began to sell – some analysts say because of worries that the government might try to slow both overall economic growth as well as valuations in the exchanges.

Current State of the Markets

New research on China's equity markets has focused on how effective reforms have been in shaping the institution. A study by Kato and Long (2006) examines the relationship between firms' performance and the rate of CEO turnover as a gauge of the influence of corporate governance. If a firm is performing poorly, it is expected that the company's leadership would be replaced if corporate governance is sensitive to the company's stakeholders. In the early days of equity-market development in China, with the emphasis on raising capital for state enterprises, this connection certainly would not have existed.

The authors' key performance measure, the rate of return on equity, resulted in several key findings based on data on firm listings between 1998 and 2002. First, the connection between CEO turnover and firm performance was much stronger for privately controlled firms than for state-controlled firms. This implies that equity markets are behaving more like established markets in other countries as more private firms participate. On the other hand, it also suggests that the desired positive effect on state-owned listed firms is less evident. Second, firms with independent boards showed a more sensitive correlation between CEO turnover and firm performance than those without. And third, there was less connection between CEO turnover and performance if the CEO also held a position simultaneously in the controlling shareholding firm. In general the Kato-Long (2006) results support the expectation that more independence for decision-making is better for firm performance.

Another study by Shi (2006) examines how reforms to end the overhang of non-tradable shares by solving the problem of unequal investment costs have affected the value of listed companies. Using the Tobin'Q model, her paper examines 188 listed companies that had finished the first phase of reform by the end of 2005 and addressed the problem of equity division by converting the non-tradable shares into tradable ones. This research tests the relationship between the companies' value and the extent of compensation. The results show that the variation in the value of companies before and after the reform is positively correlated with the protection procedures for the tradable shareholders' compensation.

The Next Challenges

The arrangement of having non-tradable shares in China's stock market led to a series of problems that began with the inception of these markets and put public investors at a disadvantage.

The implications of the Shi (2006) study explain indirectly why the market has accepted the reform procedures this time around. Compared with previous reform procedures, this time China's government recognized that the tradable share investors needed to be compensated for higher investment costs in relation to that of the non-tradable shareholders in order for the reform to be viable. Given this, the goal of China's stock market reform is clear – it is to rearrange the originally misconstrued nature of China's stock market regime to match equity markets in other countries, where the purpose of the markets includes asset pricing and re-source allocation as well as the financing function.

The implications of the Kato-Long study (2006) are that corporate governance reforms are working in investors' favor in that governance and firm performance are increasingly linked – at least in private companies.

Despite this documented progress, the recent market volatility means that further reforms to encourage institutional investors (dividend payments, short selling, mutual and index funds, and transparency) are needed. Until these are in place, trading will tend to be driven by the natural volatility of thin markets as well as speculation, rather than fundamentals of companies or the economy (Pettis 2007).

Meanwhile, Chinese equity markets have plenty of room to grow – less than 5 percent of the population owns equities (Balfour & Roberts, 2007) – and inves-tors in China are looking to diversify beyond real estate holdings. Furthermore, loosening of international capital flows is expected to go forward in the future, such as a shift to allow Chinese investors to buy international shares of mutual funds and to allow foreign institutions access to Chinese equities on the two domestic exchanges. To date, however, most foreign investors who own shares in Chinese companies have purchased them through the Hong Kong or New York exchanges. Short-term portfolio flows into and out of China are still highly restricted. Hence, the current volatility of Chinese stocks is due to domestic fac-tors, many of which are driven by reform efforts and investor's expectations about their effect on future share values.

References:

Balfour, Frederik and Dexter Roberts (2007), "Market Mania in China," *Business Week*, 19 March, p.74.

Kato, Takao and Cheryl Long (2006), "CEO turnover, firm performance, and enterprise reform in China: Evidence from micro data," *Journal of Compara-tive Economics* 34, pp. 796-817.

Pettis, Michael (2007), "Buying into China's Volatility," *Far Eastern Economic Re-view*, Jan/Feb., www.feer.com.

Shi, Yanping (2006), "An Analysis of Increasing Companies' Value by Protecting Tradable Share Investors in China's Stock Markets," Working Paper, Univer-sity of International Business and Economics, Beijing.

Walter, Carl E. and Fraser J.T. Howie (2003). *Privatizing China: The Stock Mar-kets and their Role in Corporate Reform*. John Wiley & Sons.

Yardley, Jim (2007), "Chinese United by Common Goal: A Hot Stock Tip," *The New York Times*, 30 January, pp.A1, A10.

Zhang, Ziheng (2006), *Panorama of the Reform on the Problem of Equity Division.* Beijing: Economic & Management Publishing Houses.

Yanping Shi is Professor of Finance and Economics at the University of International Business & Economics in Beijing. Professor Shi was a Fulbright Scholar in the U.S. for the 2007-08 academic year. Penelope Prime is Professor of Economics at Mercer University and Director of the China Research Center, Atlanta, Georgia.

Report on Xinjiang's Development

John W. Garver
Vol. 5 No. 3
Fall 2006

Two weeks of travel by hired vehicle in Xinjiang during June-July 2006 left a deep impression of rapid development underway in China's westernmost region. Very large amounts of money are clearly being poured into Xinjiang to develop transportation, communication, education, and housing infrastructure, and to build Xinjiang's energy infrastructure and production. Efforts to modernize Xinjiang's agriculture are also apparent, even if they are not as breathtaking as in other sectors. In all, a coordinated effort is underway to lay a basis for accelerated development in Xinjiang.

Highway Transportation

The most dramatic developments are in transportation. Newly built or refurbished highways abound. The hard-surfaced, two-lane "Petroleum Highway" cutting across the eastern part of the torrid Takmalikan desert opened in the late 1990s. Green belts of tamarind bushes and white poplar trees run alongside its 400 kilometer length, to a width of about 30 yards on either side. The size of the saplings indicate they were only recently planted, while a placard at the north end of the highway indicates that China National Petroleum Corporation (CNPC) planted the trees in 2003-2005 at a cost of RMB 218 million. The trees would not last long in the Takmalikan without irrigation, and over 100 wells have been drilled at standard distances along the highway to supply water to the plants via Israeli-derived drip irrigation (in which perforated plastic tubes carry water to the roots of plants).

But services have not yet been built along the highway; signs warn travelers to fill up with gasoline before setting out. As the name "Petroleum Highway" indicates, the road is intended to serve as the backbone for exploitation of the Takmalikan's rich petroleum resources.

A highway built in the late 1990s also extends east of Hetian (Khotan in the old usage) linking up with the southern end of the Petroleum Highway at Minfeng. Prior to that, there was, according to locals, no modern road east of Hetian. A very good, U.S.-interstate or German autobahn-style limited-access highway has just opened extending north from Kuerle (Korla in the old style) north— a city that hosts Mobil Oil Corporation offices in the effort to exploit Takmalikan oil—to Turpan and then further north to Urumuqi, Xinjiang's capital. This provides good road access between the rail junctions at Urumuqi and Korla, at the northern end of the "Petroleum Highway."

North of Kuche, a city lying about two hundred kilometers west of Kuerle on the "northern silk road" along the edge of the Takmalikan, surveyors are at work laying out alignments for widening and improving of currently narrow roads winding through the foothills of the Tianshan Mountains. Construction equipment is being marshaled along those routes, and one old compound has been designated headquarters for the construction effort and was festooned with new signs and propaganda banners proclaiming the importance of roads for Xinjiang's development. The hard-surface highway extending north of Kuche to the ancient ruined city of Subashi ends at the entrance to that ancient ruin. Locals told me that plans are being made to push the hard surface road north through a rugged canyon to link up with the soon-to-be expanded highways north of Kuche.

A highway has been pushed over the Kyrgyz-China border at Irkestan Pass about 150 kilometers west of Kashgar. A detailed map of Xinjiang published in Beijing in 1999 did not show such a road (nor did earlier CIA-published maps I had consulted), yet the road was in heavy operation in mid-2006. Truck traffic was heavy. Scrap metal seemed to be the major commodity flowing from Kyrgyzstan to Kashgar, while Chinese manufactured goods flowed west. A large "port" has been constructed just below the great rise to the crest of the mountains on the Chinese side, where there was abundant traffic and commercial activity. Several years ago the Asian Development Bank decided to fund two trans-Kyrgyz highways—one crossing into Kyrgyzstan from China at Irkeshtan, and the other at Torugart Pass, 100 kilometers to the north.

Across Xinjiang, gas stations are opening like bamboo shoots after a spring rain. Whether because of growing market demand or government directive is unclear, but such stations are abundant. Most have that just-opened look, and many others are under construction. There is apparently sharp competition in this area between CNPC, Sinopec, and Xinjiang companies, including one affiliated with the PLA Construction and Production Corps in Xinjiang. It is not uncommon to see several filling stations within close proximity of one another.

Telecommunications

Many kilometers of fiber optic cable have been recently laid across both northern and southern Xinjiang. The paths of these cables have been marked with two-foot high, white-painted concrete markers to prevent construction crews or farmers from damaging them, and these fresh-looking markers parallel both the "southern silk road" and the "northern silk road" routes we traveled. Locals confirmed that these lines had been recently put in. There were also frequent, moderately sized, and apparently newly constructed stations along these new cable lines. I took these to be booster stations associated with the operation of the fiber optic cable. Most of these stations were emblazoned with the "China Mobile" logo. Further testament to the newness of the fiber optic cable network were frequent, and new looking, propaganda signs exhorting people to protect and respect the fiber optic cables (guang xian). Lots of new mobile phone transmission towers also were sprouting, again along both the northern and southern rims of the Takmalikan.

Education

There are many newly constructed school buildings in villages and small towns in Xinjiang. It appeared that much money and effort is going into basic education. Again current propaganda themes suggested as much. "Human talent (ren cai) is the basis for development" was a common slogan on signs and banners.

The Petroleum Industry

Large scale exploration and production activity is underway at the Lunnan oilfield east of Kuche. Dozens of pumps were in operation and visible from the highway, reminding me very much of the Oklahoma oil patches I worked as a teenager. Many of the pumps looked very fresh. New wells were being drilled— perhaps a half dozen were visible from the highway, and heavy drilling, pumping, and storage equipment was being moved about over the highways. New storage tanks have been built alongside older and smaller ones. There was intense truck activity to and from storage facilities, although some new pipelines were under construction as well. There was one large, perhaps 18-inch pipeline being laid to, or perhaps from, one of the storage facilities. An impressive, largish, and newly rigged out "Lunnan oilfield base" (Lunnan youtian jidi) was visible and advertised from the highway, apparently to organize all this activity. Over the horizon across the northern rim of the Takmalikan, railway trains of oil tank cars and coal or ore hopper cars moved at frequent intervals.

Preparations are underway to search for petroleum further into the Takmalikan, apparently in the vicinity of the new "Petroleum Highway." Along that highway were visible three parks of construction equipment, truck-mounted drilling rigs, tanker trucks, and miscellaneous heavy trucks and other vehicles. Some of these motor parks were flanked by tent compounds, apparently for the soon-to-arrive workers. The vehicle parks had a strong military look, but involvement of the PLA was not apparent. PLA men were, however, stringing new power or telephone cables along the "southern silk road" route.

Agriculture

Agricultural machinery was not abundant. There were some mechanical threshers, fans (for winnowing grain), and tractors in the fields, but much more agricultural production seemed to be based on animal or human muscle. People were threshing grain by beating it, winnowing by muscling it into the air, plowing with donkeys, or turning the soil with hoes or shovels. In Kuche a local government bureau concerns itself with agricultural mechanization. They have a rich field for activity.

Interestingly, there were many new grape trellises along both the northern and southern "silk road" routes. Common configurations were long archways leading out from the entrance of houses, or flanking one side of the house. One could ascertain recent construction from both the non-weathered character of the wood and the short size of the grape vines. Many trellises were under construction.

Apparently there is increasing demand for Xinjiang grapes. It may be that the popularity of wine along China's east coast is creating new demand and, consequently, the expanded supply of Xinjiang grapes. Local demand for grapes might be increasing as well. Over the last several years, Xinjiang Uighurs (most of whom are forbidden by Islam to drink alcohol) have established fruit juice companies that produce high quality beverages patronized by many Xinjiang Uighurs for reasons of ethnic pride. Nonetheless, it seems hard to imagine that all those new trellises are supplying local demand.

Cotton production is another area of agriculture in which there is visible new activity. Cotton is Xinjiang's major crop. There were several (a half dozen or so) newly built cotton ginning plants where seeds are removed and the raw fiber put in bales for shipment to east-coast textile centers. There was no evidence of foreign or Hong Kong investment in these facilities.

Extensive construction in villages along both the southern and northern "silk road" routes indicates growing prosperity at least in villages adjacent to highways. Houses and walls of unbaked mud and animal manure are being torn down and replaced with dwellings of fired yellow bricks. Hundreds of houses, sometimes whole sections of villages, were being rebuilt in this fashion. Trucks carting new, fired yellow bricks to and fro were abundant. Piles of yellow brick beside houses are as common as newly built houses.

Where does this prosperity come from? It is apparently not from increased productivity due to mechanization. Maybe it comes from the increased production of cash crops such as grapes? From increased government purchase prices for cotton, or reduced agricultural taxes? Aside from grapes, the other apparent cash commodity is sheep, the major item in the fabulous Kashgar animal market. A mature male sheep sold for Rmb 800 (about US$100).

Tourism

Tourism is another growth industry in Xinjiang. Many new "tourist sites" are being developed. The Han-Tang-era cemetery at Gaocheng outside Kuche has been graced with impressive gates where tickets are sold and brochures handed out, and a structure overlooking the cemetery. A "grape scenery" theme park — with admission only to motor-vehicle-borne tourists—has recently opened in Turpan. The "thousand Buddha caves" at Kirgzil north of Kuche have recently been extensively refurbished with concrete stairways and walkways to bear heavy traffic. At Kashgar, a monument has been recently built to the Han dynasty general Ban Chao and his "36 heroes," who brought the Kashgar region into the Han orbit.

While there are a fair number of Western tourists, it seems that the overwhelming majority are Chinese vacationing from elsewhere in China. At all of the tourist sites mentioned above, Chinese tourists far outnumber Westerners.

Dearth of Foreign Investment

There was little evidence of foreign investment or other commercial activity by foreign firms: no joint ventures, no advertising, no businessmen bustling about hotels. I saw one Volkswagen dealership and indication of involvement of a French geophysical company in oil exploration. As noted earlier, Mobil is also involved in oil activity. There was also the ever-present Coca-Cola and Pepsi, but not much more. The contrast between this situation and the abundance of foreign commercial activity in lower Yangtze or the Pearl River Delta was striking. It may well be, however, that the impressive improvement of infrastructure currently underway in Xinjiang will lay a basis for greater future foreign commercial interest in Xinjiang.

John Garver is Professor of International Affairs in the Sam Nunn School of International Affairs at Georgia Institute of Technology, Atlanta, Georgia.

View from China:
Is There a Consumption Problem?

Penelope B. Prime
Vol. 8 No. 2
Spring 2009

China saves, the U.S. consumes—or so the headlines say. Many analysts (including this author) have written about China's high savings rates and therefore low consumption, which reinforces China's dependence on exports for its growth.

The problems with this dependence are first that China has been so successful with exports that most major buyers cannot absorb more of them and will not be a source of future growth. Secondly, that such high exports make China's economy vulnerable to the business cycles of other parts of the world. Even before the current financial crisis, which has caused exports to decline substantially, there was a vigorous debate within China about how to stimulate domestic demand to get around these problems.

To date, very little has changed in China in terms of policy or institutions to address the domestic demand issue in sustainable ways. To be fair, the global financial crisis has caught the attention of policy makers everywhere, putting short-term fixes out front. Stimulus packages are popular, and China has its own version, which in essence means funding infrastructure projects combined with low-cost loans via the banking system for other government construction projects. Subsidies for rural families to buy consumer goods and a tax cut on auto sales have also been made available, but there is little evidence yet that many have taken advantage of the offers. The stimulus may be working to keep growth afloat, but in terms of changing the domestic-external demand imbalance, something more will be needed.

So what might that be? Thinking through this question from the view of a typical family in China sheds some light on the nature of savings and consumption in this transition economy. Savings is defined as earned income minus consumption in a given year. Three aspects of how a family participates in China's impressive growth and development could be thought of as: 1) access to a better life; 2) worries about losing that better life; and 3) defining what it means to have a "better life." The focus here is an average family, not one that has ties to government or party that provides access to exceptional opportunities. Some people in this second category live very well indeed, but their choices about employment, spending and saving cannot explain the overall trends in China's economy.

Access to a better life

If a person has a wage-paying job, i.e., a formal job that earns a monthly paycheck, there is a base wage that has risen with growth in China's economy but still is considered basic pay. For an employee working on the line in a factory near Beijing, for example, that base pay averages 1,200 RMB to 2,000 RMB per month ($177 to $294). In addition, most people receive an annual bonus at Chinese New Year that equals one month's pay or more. Many people do extra jobs or work overtime for extra pay. In addition, both spouses in a married household are likely to work, increasing the options and income.

In the countryside, if a farming family is able to raise and sell a cash crop or has a small, side business such as trucking or running a store or restaurant, they can do better than subsistence. If a family member ventures out and finds a wage-paying job in the city, the family usually receives part of this income as well, especially once a year at Chinese New Year when the family member returns for a week or more.

Another way an average person can share in China's growth is to speculate in the domestic stock market. Since dividends are not paid on shares, making money in the market means being lucky enough to buy low and sell high, and hence the stock market is not considered a long-term investment. Some people have made extra money—sometimes substantial amounts—in the market. One difference between families in China and families in the U.S. in this regard is that Chinese families usually think of their market investments as money that is not essential for living. The market is for making an extra gamble that may or may not pay off, if they have money to lose. Many families continue to hold savings in cash in bank accounts rather than using their basic savings to buy stocks.

Borrowing to spend is not common or easy. Base wages generally cover necessities, and any extra income earned via bonuses, second jobs, remittances or stock market winnings is most likely treated as a lucky addition, and, according to economic theory, a higher proportion of this income is probably saved as compared with the basic monthly income, at least for some time. Once savings have accumulated, they are often spent on big-ticket items such as a condo or a car, a child's tuition, or one's own or a family member's expenses after retirement.

One way that a generation of people came into wealth in China is related to housing reform. Before reform, people working in urban areas were assigned apartments by their employers. These apartments were owned by the enterprises or institutions they worked for, and so if they paid rent, it was very low. The apartments were part of the benefit package supplied under the former socialist system. As a first step in housing reform, government enterprises and institutions sold residents their apartments at highly subsidized rates. For example, a one-bedroom apartment in Beijing now worth $100,000 might have cost just $10,000.

While some people have sold their condos, casual observations suggest that most have not. In fact, many families have saved money and then bought a bigger condo, keeping their older ones as an investment, to rent out, sell later or hold for their child when they will need a place to live to start a family. Surprisingly, many families earning basic wages of even 5,000 RMB ($735, or $1470 if both spouses work) per month own 2 to 5 condos, sometimes in multiple cities. The value of this real estate must be enormous, and represents "locked-in" savings not currently available for consumption.

People from small towns, inland areas or the countryside often create their own wealth by moving to urban areas to try their luck with a small business. Fast-food stands, flower stalls, a space at Beijing's famous Hongqiao or "Pearl" market, are some examples. Local residents also open restaurants and other family companies. These companies need to bid for a license or permit to locate on a particular street or have a booth in one of the markets. They can often make a decent living in terms of generating income for their families this way.

The Uncertainties of a Better Life

However, the uncertainties built into these new income-generating opportunities are high. Change in China is very fast. Policy changes affect how one does business, and neighborhoods are frequently demolished for the next high-rise. Both can quickly end the fortunes of the small business owner. The lesson is to earn as much as you can as fast as you can, and save most of it so you can start again when needed. Every several years neighborhoods can change almost completely in terms of the restaurants and stores that are open, the vendors that are around selling snacks and fruit, and basic services such as dry cleaning and phone cards. Whole streets of businesses have disappeared within days when a new construction project was begun. With the lack of insurance policy options, saving for these rainy days must be a priority for most people.

Among other major, uncertainties that are officially recognized and supported by research is the need for families to save for unexpected health expenses, education and retirement. The previous versions of these social services and systems from the time of Mao's leadership were eroded with reforms, and China's policy makers are in the midst of recreating them for their modernizing society. In the meantime, however, saving for these future expenditures is one of the main drivers of a high savings rate from a household's point of view.

Further, the more that people rely on the private sector rather than state enterprises for their employment, the more uncertainty is introduced into their lives. The insecurity associated with market business cycles is something that we understand in the U.S. even if American households underestimate the risk at times. In China, however, these cycles are a new aspect of life that is part of the transition to a more market-oriented economy.

Defining a Better Life

In the midst of all the discussion of high savings and low consumption, the middle class in China seems to feel that it has much of what it needs. Families eat out at restaurants many nights in a week; they have plenty of clothes; they are saving for or have already purchased a car; they have a place (or several) to live; they have taken more vacation trips than their parents could have even dreamed of, both within China and abroad. And so what do they want to spend their money on? Not much, it seems—except for intangibles such as good health, excellent education for their children, and security in retirement.

Creating a dynamic, domestic market would require a competitive, innovative business environment where companies would seek out and create home-market niches based on new products, services and entertainment that would appeal to the Chinese consumer or business end-user or that would help reduce the uncertainties currently built into life today. This, in turn, may require more economic activity to be service and private-led, rather than manufacturing and state-led. Financial reform that allows for loans for small- and medium-sized companies, and for individuals and families, would help, as would new financial products such as basic insurance options for home, life and health.

In rural areas there are many families that cannot join the middle class with their current income options. The combination of land that is locked into state ownership, and so cannot be sold to finance new livelihoods, and the difficulties of moving one's residence due to the household registration system, keeps these families from gaining anywhere near as much as those who are lucky to live in urban areas and are educated. Chinese statistics put the average annual income of the 727 million rural residents at 4,761 RMB or $700 per year (*China Daily Business Weekly* May 18-24, 2009, p.12).

Making Buyers Out of Savers?

Some of the factors that are suppressing consumption in China today may be temporary. The locked savings in housing, for example, should be whittled away as families take advantage of their investment for their children, retirement or other big ticket items. Consumption behavior is also known to lag increases in income, which has happened for many families in China for many years. As growth rates level out, consumption spending is likely to catch up. And everyone talks about the younger generation and their willingness to spend.

The big question is whether major policy and institutional change will be required to stimulate China's domestic market, and whether these changes are feasible. Reforms might include building a competitive financial services sector, revaluing the Chinese currency (which would make exports relatively expensive and imports relatively cheaper), ending the household registration system, and adding a property tax while lowering the value added tax that keeps the prices of goods high. Or will the political base of the production sector dominate such that production-oriented policies will continue? Hopeful signs exist. Reforms targeting benefits to the average person, such as the new labor contract law, have been designed and implemented. Others, such as a national pension system and requiring listed companies to pay dividends to shareholders, are in the works.

On top of these moves, ironically, the current economic crisis, bad as it is for everyone, may give China a push to move aggressively to make the necessary changes to build a domestic-demand engine. If there was any doubt that continued export growth was questionable, the current global business environment has shown China the vulnerabilities of their past export-dependent growth.

Penelope Prime is Professor of Economics at Mercer University, and Director of the China Research Center, Atlanta, Georgia.

China's Emerging Consumer Market

What's Missing in China's Stimulus Package?

Li Qi and Rosemary T. Cunningham
Vol. 8 No. 3
Fall 2009

As the world begins to emerge from the worst economic recession in recent memory, stimulus packages enacted by various governments around the world are very much in the spotlight. The early verdict on China's massive stimulus is favorable. *The Wall Street Journal* reports that "spending by Chinese consumers is holding up pretty well, partly because of heavy stimulus spending by a government flush with cash. Urban household spending in China was up 9.2% in the first half of 2009."[1]

But will the stimulus bring lasting change?

China unveiled its 4 trillion RMB (US$586 billion) stimulus package at the end of 2008. The centerpiece of this plan is fiscal spending on public infrastructure development and social welfare. Some of the key areas include housing, rural infrastructure, transportation, health and education, environment, industry, disaster rebuilding, income-building, and tax cuts. The massive scale of government spending was visible everywhere on the authors' visit in 2009 to China, such as major redevelopment work on the Bund in Shanghai.

The essence of the stimulus package is government-led spending. Government-led behavior often generates growth spurts (as confirmed by recent consumer spending figures mentioned above). This stimulus package will no doubt increase China's GDP. It is also a smart strategy to adjust an economy that relies too much on exports and too little on domestic demand. Investing in public infrastructure

---

1 Source: *"China Inc. Looks Homeward as U.S. Shoppers Turn Frugal," Wall Street Journal, September, 29, 2009. Available at: http://online.wsj.com/article_email/ SB125417559519247515-lMyQjAxMDI5NTI0OTEyNzk1Wj.html*

and the social welfare system will further strengthen domestic demand and serve the economy well in the long-run.

However, what China needs is to stimulate the more sustainable force of domestic demand - household consumption – and make sure that this new increase in consumer spending is not just a temporary growth spurt. China's households have always had a low consumption rate compared not only with advanced economies like Japan and the U.S. but also with other large developing economies such as India and Brazil.[2] In 2007, household consumption expenditures were 60.8% of GDP in Brazil and 55.0% in India but only 35.9% in China.[3] Moreover, our recent field interviews with households in Beijing, Shanghai and Xian indicate that Chinese consumers are still not buying or planning to buy more goods in the future. For example, one of our survey questions asked households: if they suddenly earn 50,000 Yuan, how they would spend the money? There were five possible options: savings or investment; pay debt; give to children or relatives or donate to social causes; buy a house, car, furniture, or electronic appliances; and spend on travel and other leisure activities. The average response was to save nearly 60 per cent of the 50,000 Yuan, instead of spending it on durable goods or vacations.

The low consumption rate to GDP poses challenges to China's new balanced growth strategy, which is focused on shifting the source of growth from export revenues to domestic demand. This low consumption rate also demonstrates that the current allocation of economic resources (a core issue to economics) is not largely determined by Chinese households. As an economy moves from a planned to a market mode, one expects resource allocation decisions to shift from the state to households or private hands. In that regard, China has a long way to go. The state still has a high command on China's economy after decades of market reforms.

Nevertheless, the stimulus package is sensible and should help increase household spending. Studies have shown that low social security and health care benefits do contribute to a low consumption ratio (Qi and Prime 2009). Households may not have to save as much for the future once a more effective and generous social welfare system is built. Moreover, this package also introduces creative ways to stimulate consumer spending. The recent 7 billion Yuan subsidy for households to trade-in outdated cars and color TVs is working to increase domestic sales.

Yet once again, what happens after the sales spurt powered by this one-time subsidy? Taking care of the future (social welfare) alleviates households' burden for retirement, but increasing current household incomes is necessary and urgent.

---

2 *Data source : World Development Indicators, based on 1990-2005 data.*
3 *Principal Global Indicators, Inter-Agency Group on Economic and Financial Statistics, accessed 5 July 2009.*

Unfortunately the stimulus package is silent on this.

Chinese people have enjoyed unprecedented income growth by virtue of the success of market reforms. Millions have been lifted out of poverty. Compared to the past, household incomes have been growing tremendously. However, investigating the composition of China's growth in income from 1997 to 2007 (the last year for which the data is available), we see that in 27 of the 31 regions identified in the China Statistical Yearbook,[4] compensation of laborers experienced the lowest average annual growth rate compared with that of depreciation of fixed assets, net taxes on production and operating surplus. In all 31 regions, the average annual growth in operating surplus is higher than the increase in compensation of laborers. On average, the growth in operating surplus exceeded the growth in compensation by 9.7 percentage points each year.

The large differential between the growth in operating surplus and compensation of laborers may also be adding to the income inequality among regions in China. The differential growth in compensation compared with the growth in operating surplus appears to be inversely related to the region's gross domestic product per capita. For example, in Guizhou, which had the lowest income per capita in both 1997 and 2007, the annual average growth in operating surplus was 18.25 percentage points higher for the 1997 to 2007 period than the average annual growth in compensation; whereas, in Shanghai, the wealthiest of the regions in both 1997 and 2007, the difference was only 0.21 percentage points. The correlation coefficient for GDP per capita by region in 1997 and the difference between operating surplus growth and compensation growth is -0.49.

Indeed, many scholars have voiced concerns over the low growth rate of laborer compensation and the small share of individual income out of overall GDP income. Wei Jie stresses that "individual income as a share of GDP has continuously been too small. Meanwhile, government tax revenue has grown faster than national GDP. The most unfair issue of income distribution is that the state has taken too much, and individuals have received too little."[5]Zheng Xi, another economist, emphasizes that to increase household consumption, ways must be found to raise household income, especially for farmers and those in the lower and middle income brackets.[6]

The Chinese government, in fact, has started to consider new policy initiatives targeted to improve overall GDP, income distribution, and household income, especially for farmers, who generally have much lower income than urban residents. One of the boldest moves is to consider land privatization in rural areas. Under a draft law set to be enacted in 2020, China's more than 800 million farmers would

4 *China Statistical Yearbook 1998 and 2008, China Data Online, accessed 5 July 2009.*
5 *Source: http://video.sina.com.cn/finance/20090413/144916044.shtml*
6 *Source: http://video.sina.com.cn/finance/20090507/144116840.shtml*

be able to trade, purchase or sell their land rights under a new land policy, which addresses the most serious grievance for Chinese farmers – violation of their land rights by corrupt local officials who often seize their land and get rich through rapid industrialization schemes.

Policies to put economic decision-making into farmers' hands are efforts to reach the government's goal to "double the per capita disposable income of rural residents by 2020."[7] Theoretically, privatization could lead to much more efficient use of China's arable land and bring economies of scale that would lower agriculture production costs. But details about how land transactions would be regulated are still being debated, and many are doubtful that farmers will truly benefit in the end. Further, this potential change years from now will not have any immediate effect on improving the very low consumption rates of poor households. Fortunately, there are some other policies in effect now that can help improve the living standards and incomes of the poor. Among them: increasing unemployment and social welfare benefits for low-income households, and training programs for unskilled labor in rural areas.

Chinese officials and scholars view the global recession as more of a golden opportunity than a threat. They see it as a chance to adjust China's economic structure domestically and their relationship to the world market. Further, the current situation confirms that their recent move to a balanced-growth strategy is not only necessary but also strategically beneficial for China's long-term development. However, determining that the source of future growth lies within domestic demand is only the first step. Stimulating and sustaining of domestic demand, which relies on increasing household consumption, is a more challenging task, which cannot be fixed by simply building more roads or bridges. In addition to establishing social welfare, China needs to balance its income distribution to channel more income to its households.

References:

China Statistical Yearbook (Zhongguo Tongji Nianjian), various years. China Statistics Press, Beijing.

Qi, Li, and Penelope B. Prime, "Market Reforms and Consumption Puzzles in China," *China Economic Review* 20.3 (2009):388-401.

Li Qi is Assistant Professor of Economics and Rosemary Cunningham is Hal & Julia T. Smith Professor of Free Enterprise, both at Agnes Scott College, in Decatur, Georgia.

7 Source: *"China Announces Land Policy Aimed at Promoting Income Growth in Countryside," New York Times, Oct. 12, 2008.*

The Plant Lady:
A Chinese Migrant's Search for a Better Life

Reiko Feaver
Vol. 8 No. 3
Fall 2009

Within walking distance of the Beijing community where I live is a strip of road brightly lined with seasonal flowers and plants from late March to October – the outdoor plant market. I have purchased my garden supplies from this market for two years and over time have developed a friendship with one that particular couple. Their story is not unusual in present-day China. But it is one many people, including those who frequent the market as much as I do, may not be awarem of. Foreign news coverage of China tends to focus on trade disputes, increased attempts by the Chinese government to exert influence in global financial and policy-making bodies, and human rights. Much less is published about the everyday life and economic opportunities of "ordinary" Chinese who will eventually shape the country's and the world's future. This article focuses on one particular family. But the experiences of my friends (whom I will refer to as the 'Plant Lady' and the 'Plant Lady's Husband') repeat themselves throughout China. They each have spent the majority of their lives away from their hometown. They have arrived where they are now through help from family. The economics of their business are common to China's vast small-enterprise economy. And their outlook on life and their financial situation is similar to that of many Chinese I know.

A Life Away from Home: Family Benefits and Burdens

The Plant Lady left her home in southern China at sixteen to wash dishes at a restaurant in the city. From there, she made it to one of the many factories in Guangzhou where she met her husband, also from the same county, and also working in a factory. From the ties formed through this marriage, she arrived in the neighborhood where I now live.

There are eight independent plant sellers in this market: three are siblings, and all are from the same county in China. The Plant Lady's Husband is one of the siblings. Each sibling has gotten established in the market with the help of a family member. The eldest brother (Dage) was the first to start selling, taking over the business of the older brother of his wife, who was successful enough to move up to wholesale plant selling. In March of 2007, Dage brought the Plant Lady's Husband with him to help. Within one month, the Plant Lady's Husband called home to his wife asking whether she thought they could sell plants. A few weeks later, the Plant Lady arrived carrying her three-and-one-half-month-old daughter. The elder sister (Dajie) is the most recent arrival. She took a loan from Dage to help start her business last year.

In China, many small economies develop around family units or people from the same hometown. One day I was sitting with the Plant Lady when a couple drove by in their three-wheel motorized cart overloaded with gardening tools. The Plant Lady told me that they were very successful because they had a brother who renovated houses and then introduced their gardening services to his clients. The Plant Lady's Husband often provides free labor to Dage, and the Plant Lady this year brought her younger brother with her because he was too "slow" and "lazy" to hold a job back home.

People from every country feel a certain affinity to those from the same area where they grew up. But, in China, these geographic antecedents carry much more weight. One of the first questions Chinese may ask each other is, "What place are you from?" This is not a question of simple curiosity. In China, cities within provinces, not to mention separate provinces, can have their own language (some refer to the differences in spoken Chinese as dialects, but, in some cases, local variations in pronunciations and word use are so great that they may be better classified as independent languages). I speak only Mandarin, the official spoken Chinese of mainland China, and the Plant Lady has to remind her daughter not to use her local language so that I can understand her. More than this, geographic origin carries with it a strong preconception of the type of person you are – whether you have a good sense of humor, whether you are trustworthy, whether you are a good businessperson, whether you are pretty. And these stereotypes, for lack of a better word, remain lodged in the back of people's minds despite long business relationships or friendships (and even among my Chinese friends who have spent many years living abroad). A common geographic origin creates an immediate bond and feeling that you know a person and what she is about. At the same time, there is a pressure to help those from your home region who are less fortunate than you. There is one seller in this plant market who comes from the same county as the

Plant Lady. She was widowed at a very young age and has never remarried. She cannot do much of the manual labor required in this business, nor does she have a car with which to make deliveries or purchase stock. Because of this, the other sellers in the market help her out. Her geographic ties allowed her to begin selling, knowing she would be backed by some measure of support. I have seen the effects of this dynamic in clothing markets where the vendors are all from the same region, and in a supermarket chain where the owner hires her workers only from her home province. I have also personally experienced it in my previous business where we sought workers from the hometown of my partner's family because their accountability to the small village back home ensured trust and responsibility.

Of course, these familial and geographic ties are not without limits. I don't think I have ever seen Dage provide free labor to his younger brother, and the Plant Lady eventually sent her younger brother home because he was too slow and lazy even to work for her. This year the Plant Lady has purchased a lawn mower. I asked her why it was not sitting there on her corner so that people would know she could mow their lawns. She patiently explained to me that she keeps it in another place. She worried that if the lawnmower were not obviously being used, other people on the strip would accuse her of wasting it and depriving them of money-making opportunities. They would use it for free and either break it or not return it. This she knows from experience: at the beginning of the season she loaned some tools to a fellow seller and hasn't seen them since.

The Small Enterprise Economy

The plant corner in my neighborhood is in some ways a microcosm of the market structure that continues to dominate China's domestic market. In a strip less than a quarter mile long, you have eight entrepreneurs selling the same or slightly varied commodities. This extreme product concentration is not limited to the least expensive items – if you want to purchase fur or leather coats, you go to the street where every shop is selling fur and leather coats; if you want computers, disk drives or memory chips, you go to the four-story building crammed with hundreds of stalls selling computers, disk drives and memory chips. The same with musical instruments, art supplies, lead pipes and plastic. Almost all the people I know who have visited China have asked the same questions I repeatedly ask myself: Why do so many individual sellers of essentially the same commodity choose to locate right next to their competitor, and how do they survive?

I am not an economist and this is not intended to be an economic article. However, I understand from friends who are professional economists that agglomeration and clusters historically occur in certain sectors in every country. Various theories have been proposed to explain this tendency, including facilitation of knowledge transfer, concentration of appropriately educated workforce, and savings from proximity to suppliers. To some extent, these theories apply in China – for instance, the higher-technology consumer goods center is located near the high-tech business and university area of the city. But even my economist friends who are old China hands tell me that current research does not adequately address the peculiarity in China of the extreme physical concentration of very small individual enterprises operated by people with the same geographic origins. From what I learned and observed through my friendship with the Plant Lady and her husband, I suggest a few additional explanations specific to China.

Word of mouth remains an important communication form. A large portion of the population still lives in small villages and towns, and this population generally has low levels of education and limited means of learning what is happening on the "outside." Concurrently, economic conditions in these areas may require that people leave in order to support themselves and their families. It is common, therefore, for people to learn of new opportunities when one person leaves and finds success, just as happened in the plant market in my neighborhood. For migrants with low levels of education (the Plant Lady finished only six years of school) and limited job prospects, it is relatively easy to step into an existing market to which they have some exposure and basic knowledge, and in which they have seen others already succeed. (Another example of word-of-mouth communication comes from my questions to the Plant Lady about where she keeps her money. She tells me that from listening to other people, she changed from hiding her money under her pillow to putting it in a bank account.)

A logical next question is why the newcomers chose to open their own small business, rather than partner with an existing business? The experiences of the Plant Lady and her husband suggest potential reasons. They spent approximately ten years working in Guangzhou, each arriving there following others from their home county. During that time, in their respective factories, each progressed quickly from ordinary factory worker to management and earned comparatively good compensation of approximately US$400 a month. Housing and food was provided, and they were able to save several thousand dollars. The factory owners liked both the Plant Lady and her husband and probably each was on the way to even more responsible and higher-paying positions. Why, then, I have asked the Plant Lady, did they leave these well-paying jobs for a business with uncertain, and potentially much lower, earning potential? She provides some concrete reasons: she and her husband saw each other only once a week; the housing was one dorm room where everyone slept on bunk beds. But the reason that seems to have made the most difference was their feeling that it was better to be their own bosses. This is a sentiment that I have heard expressed in almost every conversation I have had with Chinese people in China regardless of economic, educational, or geographic background, and regardless of age. Obviously, this is not possible for every person, but, of the people I know, a disproportionately large number either own their own business, however small, or have tried it even if they failed and had to go back to working for someone else.

The dream of being your own boss is common to many cultures. However, in China, people may be more inclined to bear the risks of entrepreneurship for more practical reasons. Although the situation is improving, workers still lack basic rights. There is no minimum, much less living, wage, and employers take full advantage by paying their workers as little as possible. An owner can be a millionaire many times over, while his workers are each taking home US$5 a day, or, at times, nothing if the owner refuses to pay. Even in larger businesses, owners exercise significant control over their workers – having full access to all e-mail and other correspondence, requiring overtime work, and managing almost every aspect of a worker's day. These realities create a level of distrust of owners and bosses and many Chinese seem to prefer to shoulder the risks that come with starting a business just to maintain control over this part of their lives.

Markets for plants and other things tend to cater to people in the immediate area. One reason is the sheer concentration of people. The plant market near my neighborhood services several complexes, but just a mile down the road is another plant market whose customers come from a different set of complexes. There are enough people living in these complexes and in the surrounding neighborhoods to support scores of sellers within a two-mile-square area. Working together with the size of the market is the difficulty of transportation in China. Despite the increase in car ownership, the majority of the population still depends on public transportation. And while China's stimulus package is helping to increase the availability of public transportation, the subways and buses remain unbearably crowded. There is a popular, rather lewd, joke in China describing a woman who gets pregnant just hopping on the bus. Even if you do have a car, the traffic conditions significantly dampen the appeal of traveling around comparison "shopping." With the unease of transportation, consumers welcome the ability to travel to just one location to purchase goods, especially combined with one final characteristic of the Chinese consumer, an obsession with bargaining.

That Chinese love to bargain is no revelation to anyone who has been to China for even one day. Certainly, one does not generally negotiate the prices at stores such as Walmart or the Chinese grocery chain Jingkelong. However, the majority of consumer purchases still occur at small businesses, and the asking prices are very rarely the price that a buyer expects to pay. "Mainstream" stores have adopted pricing practices to reflect this mentality – while there may be a price sticker, there is almost always a matching sign posting an automatic "discount." This long-standing and pervasive tradition of bargaining also means that one lives in constant dread of being cheated. Purchasing items from a place like the plant market in my neighborhood helps alleviate this fear. One is able to obtain eight price quotes in a matter of minutes. Because of the degree of competition among suppliers, the buyer has a better feeling that she is paying a fair price. The constant price negotiation also means that trust becomes very important. The Plant Lady has many long-time customers like me, and I'd bet that they come back to her for the same reasons I do. I know that if I'm a regular customer she won't cheat me. I also know that if she doesn't have something I want, she will check across the street, and if they have it, and since they know her and know that I am her good customer, they also will not cheat me. "Brand" loyalty, in a sense, may be more influential in China than it is elsewhere. In a country where there is no *Consumer Reports*, one good experience can mean a lifetime of continued purchases.

My layman's observations suggest how one tiny corner economy in China arose and perseveres: one person left; stories back home brought relatives and fellow villagers; these newcomers were limited in their opportunities but came with a strong desire to operate their own businesses; because of the limitations, it was easiest and most expedient to enter into an existing market; the population is great enough to support this market; and transportation realties and consumer buying traditions enable this market to survive. It's a situation that repeats itself throughout the city where I live and across the entire country.

Attitudes on Life

My friendship with the Plant Lady highlights some common characteristics among the Chinese people I have met – in all segments of society: self-sufficiency, generosity, humor, and optimism. In the Plant Lady's hometown, they live in the family house. It has no running water and no gas or electric stove. Cooking and heating primarily come from whatever throw-off you can find – corn husks, plant stalks, trash. In the city where I live, the Plant Lady and her husband rent a 40-square-meter room for approximately US$11 per month. But it has running water and a gas stove. I live in a townhouse that I rent for US$2,000 a month, yet I have had many conversations with the Plant Lady and her husband in which she chastises me for helping them out too much as I live a much harder life because I am on my own. To help me out, this woman gives me fresh vegetables and sells me plants practically at cost.

China remains a country largely of very frugal people, trying their hardest, and quite often succeeding, their hardest to survive and improve their own circumstances and those of their children. In her mind, with each move, the Plant Lady has made her life better. Although the money was more certain in Guangzhou, now she and her husband spend their days working together, and they can control how much and how hard to work to earn what they can. The first year she started selling plants, she jokes, they could only eat mantou (steamed bread); this year, they can eat wheat pancakes (the difference in cost being about US$0.30). Last year they used part of their savings to purchase a van (at a price less than the cost of my mountain bike, I have recently discovered) – a necessity for purchasing stock and making deliveries. This year they purchased the lawn mower. She has enough money to send her child to a private school (an institution where 50-60 children attend class together, and at night sleep in one big room watched over by one teacher, at an annual cost of approximately US$300). In the summer, her child comes to visit and enjoy new experiences. Just recently the Plant Lady announced to me that she has a new plan. Her family was outgrowing the small family house, and since the economic crisis has decreased prices, during the winter when she's back in her hometown she may take her savings and borrow from her relatives and build her own house – with a living room to entertain guests (how can friends visit you if they have to sit on your bed?) and a kitchen and a separate room for her daughter.

The media often report on the size of China's migrant working population. By some statistics, migrants can comprise up to 50 percent of the population of China's largest cities. News reports emphasize the poor conditions and lack of opportunities in China's interior with the implication that migrants have no choice other than to leave their hometowns, and that they do so reluctantly. Without doubt, the economic gap between the cities and the countryside forces people to the cities for survival. Migrant workers are easy prey for unscrupulous employers who know that without proper working permits their workers have little recourse if, for instance, they are not paid their wages. Housing conditions can be substandard and families are split apart. But whether the people who leave their hometowns are as disgruntled as often portrayed is not so clear. At least, I don't believe this is the case with the Plant Lady. (A perhaps important note here is that many educated middle- to upper-middle-class Chinese are also migrant workers and have moved to the cities from small hometowns to take advantage of greater opportunity. Very often, the families are split geographically, with the mother and father working in different cities, and the child often living in a third.)

Neither the Plant Lady or her husband, nor any of the other sellers, is getting rich. But each of them is making enough to pay their living expenses and save a little money; at least in the case of the Plant Lady and her husband, doing better than their parents, and, hopefully, providing better opportunities for their children. I asked the Plant Lady whether she wants her daughter to go to college. Of course, she says, but very few people from our town go to college; it all depends on whether she can score well enough on the entrance tests. But she has a precedent – the eldest son of her brother-in-law is in his last year of university. I asked the Plant Lady whether she would be back next year to sell plants. She says they would see: so long as the land was still empty and hadn't been taken for some other use, she would be back. If it was taken, they would look for another location. If there was no other location, they would find something else to do. That's the only thing you can do, she says.

Reiko Feaver is an attorney working in China.

China's New Labor Contract Law:
An Indian Perspective

T. G. Suresh
Vol. 7 No. 3
Fall 2008

China's new labor contract law, adopted by the National People's Congress in June 2007 and put into force in January 2008, is a landmark in the effort to achieve better labor standards in the country. It can easily be called the most enabling legal instrument for Chinese workers introduced since the start of the reforms three decades ago. Interestingly, its passage came at a time when China's cost-advantage-driven manufacturing miracle was entering into a critical juncture.

Before examining the new law and its possible implications for firms and workers, it would be useful to recall the background of its origin. Toward the late 1990s there was an intensifying trend of worker strikes and protest demonstrations across China. The contentions between workers and enterprise managers were centered on issues such as arbitrary layoffs, low wages, payment arrears, employment insecurity, managerial high-handedness and denial of social security entitlements. The workers' complaints reflected their growing anxieties about the shrinkage of livelihood rights in post-reform China. It is also widely known and well documented that Chinese workers, especially in the export-oriented manufacturing sectors in the coastal economic zones, are often subjected to a range of severe labor conditions including long working hours, low wages, pressure for overtime, shop floor violence and extremely poor living conditions in the work dormitories.

In the absence of any legal right to organize or collectively bargain, Chinese workers confronted serious challenges in securing a minimum living standard in the new market economy. The official All-China Federation of Trade Unions (ACFTU), the monopoly labor union in the country, has been assigned to promote the objectives of the reforms and therefore most often finds itself on the management side of worker-management conflicts. Local governments are more concerned with attracting investments into their region, often by promoting a labor-cost advantage, than with working to improve the lives of workers. Given these official propensities to favor investment capital, attending to worker complaints was not a high priority for local governments or their labor bureaus. Under these situations, growing worker discontent broke into open conflict with firms and local government, at times developing into low-intensity social unrest in many cities. This seems to have forced the Chinese government to acknowledge the seriousness of the problem and formulate effective institutional responses.

The New Labor Law

The new law is designed to remove some of the grievous anomalies in the existing labor contract system that evolved in the reform era. Prior to its enactment, most firms enjoyed nearly unbounded powers in determining the terms, tenure and time of termination of workers. The 1994 labor law did not have any specific provisions for making the terms of employment a binding contract. Therefore, to achieve cost advantages, most firms, both local and foreign, employed workers for shorter and more convenient periods just to complete their production requirements. This created an extremely flexible labor regime in which workers were repeatedly hired and fired, and in that process denied any claim over employment security and other benefits.

The new law has clear provisions to regulate labor contracts by making them binding on both firms and workers and explicitly setting forth rights, obligations and liabilities. The most important provision is that firms must conclude a written contract with workers; it lays down that only a written contract can establish a labor relationship. The law implies that the earlier practice of informal employment, in which workers were inducted into the production process without registering them and recording their work and remuneration cannot continue. Henceforth, employment requires a written contract that must contain details concerning remuneration, job description, working hours, and social insurance, among other things. This provision is a very significant step toward achieving minimum labor standards in China as it provides basic safeguards against labor violations arising from a lack of regulation.

At the same time, the government has recognized the varying labor requirements of companies and has provided scope for flexible employment. This has been achieved by delineating the limit and scope of specific labor needs as having separate categories of contract employment, with different claims and entitlements. The law has provided for three types of labor contracts: fixed-term contracts for limited tenure, non-fixed-term contracts for longer and unspecified periods, and a project-based contract for short-term employment.

This categorization of contract employment into three distinctive types recognizes the existing labor-market segmentation, which in turn will give ample institutional leverage for companies. Furthermore, it reflects a careful approach that avoids any strong legal claim for employment security and permits enterprises to determine the strength of their workforce based on competitive concerns. By insisting on a written contract, the new law attempts to provide protections against violations and abuses that were widespread under the earlier system. In that sense it is only a limited intervention.

As such, the new law does not encourage labor market rigidities as has been argued by some foreign firms and industry associations. The legislative intent is limited to removing some of the gross anomalies in the earlier system. For instance, Article 9 by implication forbids companies from collecting residential identification cards or other papers from laborers as collateral when hiring. This will free both migrant and local workers from involuntary attachment to companies that have in the past sometimes used their most important legal documents as bargaining chips.

For employees who have been working in a company for many years, the new law extends certain legal protections. Article 14a stipulates that a laborer who has been working in a company for a consecutive period of 10 years is entitled to a non-fixed-term contract. This type of labor contract ensures relative employment security as it does not stipulate a termination date. The same is also applicable to those workers who are less than 10 years away from the statutory retirement age.

It appears that there has been a general weakening of China's public institutions in recent years. In the context of accelerating reforms and rapid economic growth this has been particularly the case with the country's regulatory institutions. On the one hand, there has been a deliberate policy orientation to facilitate speedy investments and transactions. But on the other hand, effective regulation has become elusive in a range of areas. Many companies found they could easily circumvent or flout existing administrative (guidelines and even clear rules) with little interference from the local authorities. The provision for a written contract in the new law also faces the same challenge. In an apparent attempt to make this provision foolproof, the law stipulates that if a firm fails to sign a written contract within one year from the time of hiring, the unit will be deemed to have already signed a non-fixed-term contract with the laborer. The clarity of this clause and the prospect of penalty implied here may become effective deterrents to those firms who will still try informal employment.

Among the contentious issues that provoked labor protests in the past were layoffs and arbitrary reduction of the workforce. The new law has addressed this question by prescribing certain guidelines. The government seems to have taken into account circumstances that make it necessary for the firm to reduce existing work force and render a labor contract non-performable. Enterprises that are in difficulties such as bankruptcy-related restructuring or changes in production scales can lay off 20 persons or more under Article 41. Here it seems that the law is more sensitive to the competitive concerns of the firms as it quietly endorses management prerogatives by conceding the need for staff reduction owing to "adjustments of managerial operation style." By defining the circumstances of workforce reduction in the broadest possible range which include, in addition to the above, "major changes in the objective economic circumstances," the government has conceded a great deal of autonomy to the firms and investors. An enterprise can lay off a significant number of workers whenever it deems necessary by taking refuge in Article 41.

During the public debate on the draft law it was strongly argued by labor activists and the ACFTU that such staff reductions must require prior agreement by the company's union. However, this demand did not make it to the final text, which contains a prescription that firms shall explain only the circumstances to their union and report the staff reduction plan to the labor administration department. This suggests that neither the trade union nor the local labor bureau has any meaningful say in firm-level staff reductions and layoffs. Here again we see that the Chinese government has given substantive leverage to management and investors in strategizing their workforce deployment.

A potentially important provision provided in the new law is recognition of the concept of collective bargaining. Chapter 5 incorporates a special provision for collective contracts between enterprises and employees reached after negotiations. Labor unions are assigned to execute collective contracts on behalf of the employees. The potential scope of this provision will be steeply curtailed by two prevailing factors. First, China does not recognize any independent labor union, and in recent years all the initiatives to form independent labor unions have been nipped in the bud. The All-China Federation, even though it is the only official union, does not enjoy any meaningful organizational autonomy and is strictly subordinated to the Communist Party's overall policy framework. Therefore, a significant section of the Chinese workforce is much less sure that the Federation can genuinely represent worker interests. Second, labor unions are not allowed in the majority of the foreign firms. In recent years allegations of widespread labor abuse at firms with leading global brands and their contracting suppliers have come into sharp focus. There is a growing sensitivity toward this issue. Without independent labor unions, the idea of collective bargaining will have only notional relevance. To have any practical consequences, the government must recognize independent unions and allow them in foreign-owned firms.

An Indian Perspective

From an Indian perspective, three key points concerning the Indian case may well be useful for understanding the contrasting scenarios prevailing in the two countries. First, India's labor laws are a collection of specific statutes enacted over half a century that concern separate areas such as industrial disputes, minimum wages, labor contracts, social security and so on. Since the legislative matters pertaining to labor involve power sharing between central and state governments, great variation exists in labor standards across states in India. These labor laws are applied mainly in what is called the formal or organized sector, the bulk of which is composed of state-owned enterprises and public institutions. However, they cover only a small fraction (around 7%) of the total labor force in the country. While employees in state-owned institutions and formal sector industries are covered under the protective regulations, and therefore enjoy relative employment security, better wages and other social security benefits, laborers in the unorganized sector do not receive any protection at all. Well over 90% of the estimated 406 million workers in India do not get even the statutory minimum wages provided by legislation let alone other benefits. Why India failed to secure minimum protection for its vast laboring masses – notwithstanding progressive legislation, trade unions and a democratic polity – is an extremely confounding question.

Secondly, for all practical purposes, it is extremely difficult for an ordinary worker in India to access the institutions of labor protection. One of the main reasons for this general exclusion of workers from the institutions of labor is the excessive legalism in the working of the labor laws. This is again complicated by time-consuming procedures involving a multitude of administrative and legal offices. An attempt to seek justice can push an Indian laborer into a labyrinth of administrative and legal procedures that cannot be settled in a short time. The reality is that the Indian justice system is just not affordable for poor litigants.

Thirdly, in marked contrast with China, India has not introduced a single new piece of legislation on labor since the country started economic reforms in 1991. Even though all earlier labor laws are in force, the reforms have introduced, and of late increased, flexible employment even in organized sectors. In order to accelerate reforms and attract more investment, the government has weakened the existing machinery of labor regulations such as the office of the labor inspectorate. In addition, post-reform India is witnessing a trend of competitive federalism where state governments are competing with each other for investment and opportunities for industrialization by projecting the existing low wage rate as a comparative advantage.

China's new labor contract law, when viewed from the Indian experience, offers far greater scope in ensuring better labor standards. Although it serves to reinforce the imperatives of the new market economy by legalizing flexible labor regimes, it tries to extend minimum protective coverage to all workers, including the migrant laborers. This seems to be the real strength of this new law – that irrespective of the nature of employment every worker is entitled to a minimum wage and social security benefits. For India the inclusive nature of the Chinese law presents a vitally important lesson. As indicated above, the vast majority of India's laborers are practically excluded from the purview of existing law. The main reason for this situation is the absence of a clear law that provides comprehensive coverage to all workers. The existing laws are too fragmented, focused on separate categories of workers such as permanent employees, contract workers, apprentices, and the like. A national law applicable to all enterprises (including state-owned enterprises, private businesses, and foreign firms as is the case with China's new law) would be more effective as a legal instrument. China's new law would be the latest instance of the country's transition to a unified national legal framework that will progressively replace the earlier administrative regulations and laws concerning labor.

Some provisions in the new law are designed to remove the sources of the unfair labor practices by firms rather than targeting them when they occur, as in the case of the Indian labor laws. For instance, Article 19 stipulates periods of probation according to the length of a contract. It also prescribes that an enterprise may stipulate only one probation for any given worker. This can preempt the creation of dual labor markets within firms as practiced by some large companies in India. For example, the Hyundai Motor plant in Chennai and some leading automobile components suppliers in the region have a disproportionately large segment of short-term workers. They are employed as probation workers, apprentices, contract workers and so on for many years at drastically reduced wages.

For India, however, adopting a similar law, which in effect would legalize casual and flexible employment, would not be a useful alternative. China's reforms have come a long way and have produced better outcomes both in terms of poverty reduction as well as employment creation and increasing income. India has a long way to go in achieving similar social and economic transformations. Therefore, labor reforms in India cannot begin with the same market economy imperative that guides the Chinese labor law.

T. G. Suresh is Assistant Professor at The Centre for Policy Studies, School of Social Sciences, Jawaharlal Nehru University, New Delhi.

U.S. – China Differences and
Their Effects on Business Behaviors

Guanming Fang
Vol. 7 No. 1
Winter 2008

China may be the second largest trading partner of the U.S.,[1] but the road to this increasingly close relationship has not been smooth. There have been a lot more failures and struggles in these cross-border business interactions than successes. Although it is probably true in the business world as a whole that there will be more failures than successes, the vast difference between the U.S. and China has played a major role in the struggles and failures in U.S.-China business transactions. Understanding and adapting to differences cannot guarantee success, but it can make the venture a little easier.

Until about five years ago, most U.S.-China transactions involved U.S. direct investment in China, sourcing from China, or outsourcing manufacturing to China. Besides Hai'er, which established a manufacturing facility in South Carolina in 1999, there was practically no noticeable investment activity from China in the U.S. And even Hai'er was not a recognizable name to most Americans. That changed in 2005 when Lenovo, a Beijing-based personal-computer maker, made its historic acquisition of IBM's personal-computers division. In 2006, Georgia saw its first direct investment from a Chinese manufacturer. Ningbo Lehui Food Machinery Co. Ltd., headquartered in Ningbo, Zhejiang Province, formed a joint venture with New Jersey-based W.Y. Industries, Inc. in Newnan, Georgia, to manufacture soy sauce and other condiments. In 2007, two more Chinese

---

1 Note: Includes trade in goods only. http://www.census.gov/foreign-trade/top/
dst/2007/09/balance.html.

companies called Georgia home: Wenzhou-based General Protecht Group announced it would build an assembly and distribution facility for electrical products in Barnesville, Georgia; and Changsha-based Sany Heavy Industry Co., Ltd. announced it would build an assembly plant for construction machinery, and its North American headquarters, in Peachtree City, Georgia.

With this new wave of cross-border transactions coming from China to the U.S., the differences between the two countries now affect not just those who choose to do business in China. They affect a much larger group of people, including American government officials, companies that do business or are looking to do business with the investing Chinese companies, the communities the Chinese employees and executives live in, people employed by the Chinese companies, people who are neighbors to the Chinese, and many more. Differences also impact the investing Chinese companies and the people they bring from China.

It is easy to say that the U.S. and China are different. But what are the differences? What are some of the causes of these differences? And how do they affect a company's or an individual's business behaviors? This article explores these questions, with the belief that understanding differences will make it easier to adapt to them.

Different Political Systems

China has a centralized political system. The structure of government agencies is vertical, from the central government to provincial and local governments. Within the same agency, authorities at lower levels are structurally subordinate to higher levels. A decision made at a higher level is supposed to be binding on the lower levels. For example, the decision to make Shenzhen in Guangdong Province a Special Economic Zone was made at the top leadership level, without any local input. Once the decision was made, the local government's role was to implement that order.

This is not to say that rules and regulations promulgated by the central government will be faithfully implemented at the local level. Quite the contrary. Because of the size of the country and the distances to the central government agencies in Beijing, among other things, local government agencies may well decide what to enforce (or not to enforce) and how to interpret rules and regulations they decide to honor. Nonetheless, if a higher level government decides to undertake a project and strongly communicates that decision to the local government, the local government has an obligation to implement that decision. On the other hand, the U.S. follows a federalist system, in which power is shared between the federal government and the state governments, each enjoying its own authority within the federal framework. This is also true between state government and local governments. State governments do not have authority over certain matters that are exclusively reserved within the jurisdiction of local government, such as land use.

This difference may be puzzling to a Chinese company that has been interacting primarily with state officials at the early stage of negotiating its investment in the U.S. when it realizes later in the process that it has to "re-negotiate" the details of certain matters with the local government. Following the practices in China's centralized political system, they wonder why the state cannot simply tell the local government what to do. On the other hand, this request would be incomprehensible to the state and local government officials, who understand the limits and boundaries of their authority. Efforts made on the state's part to mediate discussions between a Chinese company and a third party, such as a landowner or a local government agency, can be misunderstood as negotiations with the state. It is hard for a Chinese company to understand that with regard to matters that are outside the state's jurisdiction, the state has no authority to make binding decisions.

Different Roles of Government

China is, in theory and to a certain extent in reality, a Communist country. Until as recently as ten years ago, the vast majority of the country's business enterprises were owned by the state. There was practically no line between government and business. Although China's economy, to a large extent, has been privatized in recent years, the government and Communist Party still maintain strong control and influence over many business activities. Such control is usually reflected in the many layers of regulatory approvals that businesses are subject to. Also, historically, China is a country ruled by men rather than by law. A man of power can greatly influence a company's business decisions and its chance of success. Although China's legal system has improved significantly in the last decade, it is still immature and inadequate for the country's fast-growing economy. People are still learning to rely on the legal system to protect their personal and business interests. The result of this transitional status of China's legal system is that the government has broad discretion in implementing rules and regulations and in making decisions.

Chinese businesses are accustomed to relying on good relationships with government officials to get things done. With this mindset, dealing with U.S. government officials can be frustrating to the Chinese. For example, if Chinese investors encounter obstacles in their negotiation with a private party regarding a specific matter, they would naturally expect the state government officials who recruited them to help resolve the issues. They might have a difficult time understanding that the state officials' powers are limited by law and that, even with the best intention to help, state officials cannot always direct private business decisions. The frustration is often mutual. From the state officials' perspective, they do not understand why they are called upon and put into the middle of an issue that should be negotiated and resolved between private parties.

Different Legal Systems

While China, under Communist rule, has always had a criminal justice system, the civil legal system has a history of less than 30 years. Modern China did not have any law program in universities until the late 1970s. China did not have any trained lawyers until the early 1980s, when this first class of law students graduated.[2] Judges with formal legal training came even later. Without the protection of a functional legal system, Chinese people traditionally relied on relationships, trust and gut instincts to protect their personal interests. In connection with China's accession to the World Trade Organization, China started a major reform of its legal system in the 1990s. According to the All China Lawyers Association, a self-disciplined professional association, China has about 110,000 lawyers today.[3] Although this number is insignificant compared to the number of lawyers in the U.S., particularly given the population disparity, this is a significant jump from the 5,500 lawyers that China had in 1998.[4] Moreover, according to an article recently published by *Business Week* online,[5] in the years between 2001 and 2004, China promulgated more than 94,000 laws and regulations, almost tripling the new laws and regulations from the previous five years.

Despite these significant improvements, when compared to the U.S. legal system, China is still in a toddler stage. Many laws have not had an opportunity to be applied, interpreted and enforced. Many lack meaningful mechanisms for implementation and enforcement. Many conflict with each other. Compared with the size of the population and the economic growth of the country, the number of lawyers is severely inadequate. Moreover, China's judicial system has not caught up with the demands of the country's rapid economic development or the development of the written laws. There are still many judges who do not have formal legal training. Relying on the legal system to protect one's personal and business rights is still a new concept to many in China and can be a risky proposition. As a result, handshakes, trust and gut feelings continue to play a major role in forming business relationships. Understanding a legal contract is different for the Chinese

---

2 *Law programs are undergraduate programs in China.*

3 *http://www.acla.org.cn/html/union/englishunion/briefintroduction.html.*

4 *"China's Legal System: A Bum Rap?" by Randall Peerenboom, http://www. international.ucla.edu/article.asp?parentid=2878.*

5 *"Debunking Myths about China's Legal System," by Steven Dickinson, http:// www.businessweek.com/globalbiz/content/nov2007/gb20071129_851610. htm?chan=search.*

and for the Americans. For the Chinese, a contract creates a platform upon which a relationship will be built, rather than boundaries of the relationship. U.S. companies and governments often get requests from their Chinese counterparts to enter into memoranda of understanding, which are usually non-binding. While the Chinese attach great significance to these memoranda, viewing them as an announcement of a formal relationship, their U.S. counterparts usually regard them as goodwill, mere ceremonial documents. There has been much complaint that Chinese companies do not respect binding contracts. There is no doubt that dishonesty and unethical business behaviors are partly to blame for the problem, but another part of the cause is the different understanding of the role a contract plays.

Cultural Differences
Hierarchy

Cultural differences often color business behaviors. In China, schools of philosophy that originated in ancient times can influence the sense of morals and virtue today. For example, Confucianism, which was developed between 500 and 400 BCE, teaches that every person has a "proper position" in society. Confucianism emphasizes personal and governmental morality, correctness of social relationships, justice and sincerity. This philosophy explains, at least partially, why there is usually a strong sense of hierarchy within a Chinese entity or organization. Authorities are clearly delineated internally, and respect appropriate for each position is expected. Consider an example of how this cultural difference affected the business behavior of a Chinese company. Recently, the company had an opportunity to be showcased in some photographs that would appear on a conference brochure. The conference would be attended by hundreds of prominent business, political and community leaders from the company's new locale. This would have been a great opportunity for the company to gain significant publicity and recognition among an influential group of people. However, the company turned down the opportunity. The reason is simple and perhaps incomprehensible to Americans. The president of the company was unavailable during the time of the photo shoot, and the vice-president did not think it would be appropriate for him to appear without his boss in photos representing the company.

In most private Chinese companies, ownership is highly concentrated in one person or a handful of people. These owners have total decision-making power. But they are not always involved in transaction negotiations, which are usually handled by lower-level officers, who may not be in direct contact with the owners. As a result, decisions may be made with incomplete or misinterpreted information. As more information is obtained, these decisions may be modified. For the U.S. parties involved in the negotiation, their Chinese counterparts may appear indecisive and unreliable. The U.S. side may not know whether an issue discussed and thought to be agreed upon at the negotiation table will later be changed.

From a Chinese company's perspective, entering the U.S. market involves more than hiring a team of competent employees, building up a sales network, and establishing sales channels. It also means adjusting to a different culture. Executive officers who are used to being addressed properly by their titles now hear themselves called by their first names by their American business partners and customers, and even employees. They will no longer have a personal driver, which is a standard perk for many executives in China. Companies that enjoy dominant positions back home will often find that they are now just one of many companies in the U.S. And more important, they will be learning a new way of building relationships (less wining and dining, more exchanging of information), the workings of a different political and legal system, and how to use the U.S. legal system to protect their rights.

Gender Equality

Because of decades of isolation between China and the United States, there are a lot of misconceptions in the U.S. about the role of women in China's business world. U.S. companies often wonder whether it is appropriate to send their female executives to the negotiating table and whether hiring qualified Chinese women for management positions would hurt their chances of success in China.

According to the Confucian teaching, a girl should defer to her father, a wife to her husband, and a widow to her son. On the other hand, Confucianism also teaches filial piety toward one's parents, including the mother. As a result of these seemingly contradictory teachings, in ancient China women had little, if any, decision making power, even though they were highly respected and even worshipped by their children, and their desires were usually followed by their sons. Women's roles in society obviously have evolved significantly since Confucius' days. When the Communist Party took over China in 1949, Mao Zedong proclaimed that "women hold up half the sky." Women's equal rights are protected by the Chinese constitution. Women stopped taking their husbands' name when Dr. Sun Yet-sen overturned the Qing Dynasty in 1911, long before the Communist takeover. Women started working outside their homes in large numbers in the 1920s. Today, women work in most, if not all, professions and occupations in China. Many successful entrepreneurs are women. However, Chinese women face the same glass ceiling that U.S. women face. The number of women in top leadership positions is extremely low given the size of the population. Habits from thousands of years ago die hard. There is still an unspoken, and sometimes unintentional, belief that, at a certain level, women are inferior and less intelligent, and that being naïve is a virtue for women.

However, this does not mean that Chinese businessmen would not respect a female counterpart. Because of this unspoken belief that women are inferior, Chinese men usually do not expect much of women, perhaps unknowingly. But when a woman succeeds in what she does, she gains higher respect from men, compared to men in her position. For example, while it is unremarkable if a man is a lawyer, a woman lawyer would be considered outstanding and would earn added respect from men. One may call this a disguised form of discrimination. In the context of business dealings, one who understands this perception can use it to advantage.

Adapting to the Differences

There is no question that China will continue to be a major player in the world economy. China has a population of over 1.3 billion. Although its gross domestic product has been enjoying continuous fast growth that no other country has ever experienced, its per capita GDP is far below that of the U.S. and many developed countries.[6] On the other hand, the U.S. is undeniably a superpower in terms of economy, technology, financial sophistication, and many other aspects. The U.S. needs the consumer market that China has the potential to offer, and China needs the capital, technology and other intangibles that the U.S. has to offer. Despite the many difficulties that people have encountered and will continue to encounter, business interactions between China and the U.S. will continue. To a certain extent, they depend on each other to continue their economic growth. Business people on both sides of the ocean will have no choice but to try to adapt to the differences of the other country if they want to stay competitive and be part of this inevitable bilateral cooperation. Adaptation starts with understanding.

Guanming Fang is a Partner at Womble Carlyle Sandridge & Rice, PLLC, Atlanta, Georgia.

---

6 *The World Factbook of the Central Intelligence Agency indicates that China's per capita GDP for 2006 was estimated to be around $7,800, while the U.S. per capita GDP for 2006 was estimated to be $43,800. https://www.cia.gov/library/publications/the-world-factbook/index. html.*

China's New Science & Technology Strategy: Implications for Foreign Firms

Denis Fred Simon, Cong Cao and Richard P. Suttmeier
Vol.6 No.2
Spring 2007

According to "Science, Technology and Industry Outlook" released in late 2006 by the Organization for Economic Cooperation and Development, China has become the world's second-largest spender on research and development. Its R&D expenditures reached $136 billion in 2006 in purchasing power parity terms, ahead of Japan's $130 billion, although it is still less than half the U.S. spending of $330 billion (OECD 2006). The purchasing power terms are controversial and maybe misleading. According to the Chinese source, the 2006 R&D expenditures were only RBM294 billion ($37 billion). Nonetheless, these statistics represent an appreciable first step toward achieving one of the quantitative objectives set up by China's Medium and Long-Term Plan for the Development of Science and Technology (2006-2020). Launched by the Chinese government in early 2006, the plan is intended to turn China into an innovative nation by 2020, Its quantitative objectives include:

- Investing 2.5% of its increasing gross domestic product in R&D
- Raising the contributions to economic growth from technological advances to more than 60%
- Limiting dependence on imported technology to no more than 30% of value added
- Becoming one of the top five countries in the world in the number of invention patents granted to Chinese citizens and in the number of citations of Chinese-authored scientific papers.

While the purchasing power figure must be used with care, and while China's R&D expenditures as a percentage of its GDP – 1.41% in 2006 – has not yet reached that of a world leader in research and innovation, the underlying trend is that Chinese R&D spending has been growing by an impressive average of more than 20% over the past decade and faster than that of GDP (NBS and NBS/MST). The last several years also have witnessed the increasing role of enterprises in China's national innovation system; their contributions to the nation's R&D expenditures now account for about two-thirds of the total. Apparently, China will spend considerably more over the next 15 years, as mandated by the medium and long-term plan.

Moreover, the essence of the plan is that science and technology will drive China's future economic development, thus enabling the PRC to "leapfrog" into positions of leadership in emerging fields such as information technology, biotechnology and nanotechnology. The Chinese objective is nothing less than to put in place a national capability for promoting "indigenous innovation." The plan also introduces a policy framework for implementation of a series of new regulations and initiatives to support indigenous innovation, including providing preferential treatment for 1) innovation within domestic enterprises, government purchases, high-tech exports, and the assimilation of foreign technology; 2) encouraging foreign corporate R&D activities in China; and 3) strengthening intellectual property protection for Chinese innovators. In a word, the potential impact of the plan will be to shape the current and future trajectory of Chinese technological and economic development.

What does the plan mean to the development of the business environment and the operations of multinational corporations in China?

Reducing technological dependence

To begin with, "indigenous innovation" (zizhu chuangxin, also translated as "independent" or "homegrown" innovation) not only has become a buzz term but also has led to considerable confusion inside China and abroad because, in its ambiguity, it has been construed by some as echoing techno-nationalist notions of self-reliance (zili gengsheng) from the Maoist period – when Chinese research and innovation activities were largely cut off from the international community and experienced significant retardation as a result. In explicating the concept, however, the plan points to zizhu chuangxin as having three components: genuinely "original innovation" (yuanshi chuangxin), "integrated innovation" (jicheng chuangxin, or the fusing together of existing technologies in new ways), and "re-innovation" (yinjin xiaohua xishou zaichuangxin), which involves the assimilation and improvement of imported technologies.

Closely related to the emphasis on indigenous innovation is one of the quantitative objectives of the plan, noted above, to reduce China's dependence on imported technology to less than 30%. Here, the dependence of a nation on foreign technology is calculated by dividing the value of imported technology by the nation's domestic R&D expenditures plus the net technology exports, that is, the value of the technologies exported minus the value of technologies imported. This formula is a bit odd, and indeed, represents a Chinese "indigenous innovation" in the study of science & technology and innovation policies. On its face value, the dependence on foreign technology can be limited by either increasing domestic R&D expenditures and technology exports, or decreasing technology imports, or a combination of both.

Unfortunately, reality is much more complicated than the theory suggests. Boosting R&D spending is one thing, but turning R&D into innovative products that are competitive domestically and internationally is quite another matter. Many Chinese firms do not possess sufficient human and financial resources to engage in large-scale innovation activities – only about a quarter of China's large and medium-sized enterprises have science & technology centers, and less than 40% are engaged in S&T activities (NBS/MST, 2006, p.107). Therefore, at least for the time being, technology imports and other forms of technology introduction from outside China will continue to play an important role in building Chinese innovation capacity. The critical point is not whether the PRC should limit the importation of foreign technology, but whether China can harness and add value to imported technology. This, in turn, is linked to how they spend their R&D money, including that portion targeted for facilitating the absorption of foreign technology.

In fact, this objective reflects a serious contradiction inside the plan itself. On the one hand, innovation based on imported technology falls into the second component of indigenous innovation, as mentioned, and therefore significant efforts need to be devoted to the digestion and assimilation of such types of technology. The policy measures accompanying the plan also emphasize this fact. On the other hand, the plan points out that China should not depend so heavily on technology imports as the source of innovation. In fact, this contradiction most likely reflects the differences of interests between China's S&T policy makers, represented by the Ministry of Science and Technology, which advocates indigenous innovation and the reduction of foreign technology dependency, and Chinese enterprises, which, supposedly at the center of innovation, are less likely to bet on internally generated know-how from their more pragmatic, self-interested perspective. Interestingly, this apparent contradiction also has raised concerns among the international business community. A careful reading of the plan only reinforces the sense that reducing dependence on foreign technology may be more of a political slogan than a practical objective.

Attracting multinationals for R&D activities

The goal of decreasing reliance on foreign technology also appears contrary to the desire to attract more R&D activities by multinationals to China, as specified by the plan and reinforced in comments made by officials from China's Ministry of Commerce in December 2006. After China re-opened its door in the late 1970s, foreign corporations started entering China. The first to come were companies focused primarily on labor-intensive manufacturing activities in toys, clothing, and other low-end products. As China's investment environment improved, multinationals gradually moved higher value-added operations to China, not only to penetrate the huge Chinese domestic market, but also to climb the value chain by taking advantage of the effects of the learning curve in terms of the relatively higher quality but less expensive labor force in the PRC.

Since the late 1990s, multinationals have started to develop an R&D presence in China by opening research and engineering centers and collaborating with top Chinese universities. According to the statistics from China's MOFCOM, foreign corporations set up 980 R&D centers in China as of 2006, up from 24 in 1997. The number is probably overstated as there are most likely only 300 or so substantial foreign corporate R&D centers. Many so-called R&D centers are not independent but are affiliated with a specific venture's Chinese operations. Their registration with Chinese MOFCOM is designed, largely, to take advantage of the preferential treatment that the Chinese government is offering. Moreover, many such R&D efforts by foreign corporations in China are less part of a global innovation strategy and more related to the company's localization strategy – being closer to their Chinese operations and localizing products for the local market (Serger 2006). Viewed from this perspective, these R&D activities and their contribution to China's innovation efforts should not be exaggerated.

On the other hand, at least 30 large multinationals currently have more than 60 facilities engaging in innovative research in China. These centers, by Microsoft, IBM, Intel, GE, Motorola, Nokia, Unilever, Procter & Gamble, AstraZeneca, and others, represent a significant commitment by these companies; their activities cannot be explained simply by the attraction of the Chinese market. They are part of a larger global innovation reconfiguration. In such instances, multinationals are attracted by China's "brainpower" rather than Chinese brawn. Multinationals are plugging into China's talent pool, accessing high-quality researchers from domestic enterprises, research institutes, and universities to fortify their high-end scientific and engineering workforce around the world. The rapid growth of these types of R&D efforts may seem somewhat surprising in view of the bad press China receives about the problems of intellectual property rights protection. Nonetheless, it seems multinationals find the upside benefits worth the risks, even with the high degree of labor turnover in the Chinese economy.

While encouraging more and more of this type of investment, China's leadership also is concerned about whether these R&D centers will be effective instruments of technology transfer and whether they will bring technological spillovers to Chinese enterprises. As the world economy shows signs of becoming more protectionist and the benefits of globalization erode in some areas, the PRC leadership wants to move quickly to bring R&D into the country as a way to enhance access to high-end know-how. Whether this will occur, and via what vehicles and channels, are the big questions surrounding foreign R&D in China. Still, with support from the central government in Beijing, many local governments in the PRC are competing intensely with one another to attract these R&D investment projects.

Given the orientation of the plan, combined with global outsourcing trends, as long as China continues to turn out highly educated scientists and engineers, the country will be a magnet for the new R&D activities of multinationals. Consequently, there will be a restructuring and remapping of the global R&D landscape, through which China will surely be one of the beneficiaries. For one thing, high-end R&D from multinationals helps China to utilize global R&D resources. Indeed, as a whole, funding from the foreign sources has already contributed some 15% of China's R&D expenditures – presumably most from multinational corporations.

Stimulating high-tech exports

The plan also aims to further develop China's high-tech industries, including stimulating high-tech exports through tax and other incentives. Since the 1990s, high-tech exports have become an important growth engine for the Chinese economy (Figure 1). But, China's impressive high-tech trade statistics need to be scrutinized. First, while the PRC's export-oriented strategy has yielded obvious positive results, basic processing and assembling with key components from abroad for export purposes has accounted for a significant part of China's high-tech exports.

Second, China's export-led high-tech industry has been based on low labor costs and imported foreign technologies or even components. China has become a big assembly line for products made of high-tech parts from abroad plus some lower-tech domestic components. Most of the Chinese "indigenous" exports are lower-end products involving basic processing and manufacturing techniques, while imports in general are much more sophisticated. There has been a tendency for the world's leading multinationals, especially those in the information and communications technology area, to move their manufacturing facilities or outsource production to China – not because of Chinese competitiveness in technology, but largely because of its comparative advantages in labor. Clearly, China has

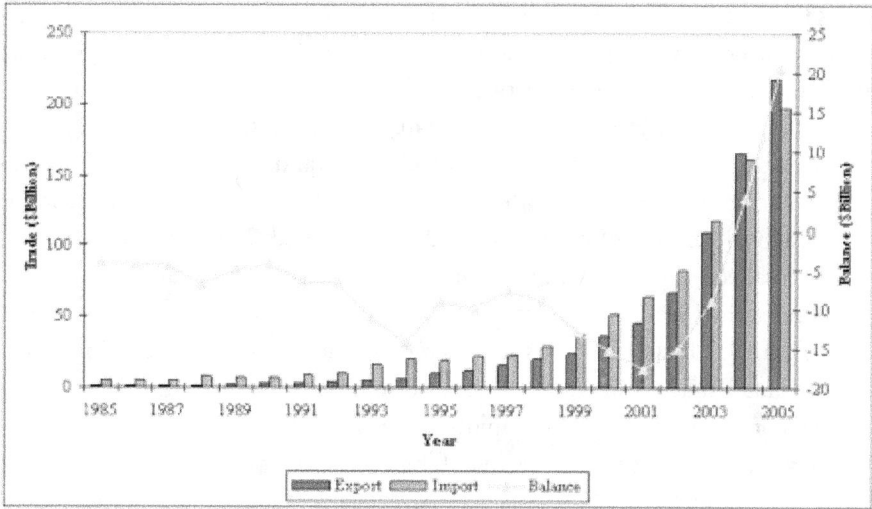

Figure 1 China's High-Tech Trade. Source: NBS/MST

moved and will further move steadily up market. Being labor-intensive, however, these types of so-called "high-tech" exports bring only a slim profit margin, sometimes as low as 2%-3%, to Chinese firms.

Third, in areas where the Chinese economy appears to enjoy a certain level of competitiveness, much of it has come from foreign-invested enterprises (sanzi qiye). Over the years, for example, most of the computer systems and mobile communications equipment have been exported by foreign-invested enterprises. Wholly-owned foreign enterprises have contributed a significant portion of China's high-tech exports – some 90% in recently years, while state-owned enterprises have seen their share decline year over year (NBS/NDRC/MST, 2006, pp.447-8).

In a word, it is high-tech multinationals that have benefited from China's increasing high-tech exports. In the meantime, China's high-tech industry remains structurally weak – emphasizing processing and assembly of low-end products with low value-added and led by foreign-invested enterprises. Because of this, China may make and export "high-tech" products in large quantity, but does not enjoy the benefits and profits that come from leveraging its own technology to produce higher value-added items. All this points to a pattern of its high demand for and reliance upon advanced foreign technology, a shortcoming that the plan explicitly wants to eradicate. And given path dependence, the domination of foreign-invested firms in China's high-tech exports poses difficulties for its domestic high-tech firms to become innovative. This is one of the reasons that the plan places so much emphasis on the building up of indigenous innovation and alleviating the dependence on foreign technology.

Strengthening intellectual property rights protection

One last point worthy of attention is the focus of the plan on strengthening intellectual property rights protection in China. This is one of the critical initiatives within China's S&T development strategy adopted in the new century – the other two being the focus on talent and technical standards – because China has paid an enormous price for overindulgence in imported technology while it has yet to establish sources of competitive advantage based on Chinese-created and -owned intellectual property rights. Furthermore, China has encountered various trade-related intellectual property rights barriers. According to a recent report in the Financial Times, China is increasingly the main target of litigation at the International Trade Commission, with the number of claims against mainland Chinese companies multiplying rapidly since 2000; foreign patent owners have won in about half of the cases against China over the past 10 years (Waldmeir 2006). Even though the Chinese have recognized the strategic value of intellectual property rights in today's global economy, they have paid a steep financial price for not understanding this point much earlier.

Protecting intellectual property rights effectively and rigorously will spur the expanded introduction of advanced technologies and especially the manufacturing of new products in China earlier in their life cycle. More importantly, intellectual property rights protection will give domestic firms incentives to invest in R&D and introduce innovative products to the market. Only when domestic entities start to be innovative is it possible for the nation to turn itself into a truly innovation-oriented society.

Conclusion

As a new, strategic S&T and innovation policy manifesto, the Medium and Long-Term Plan for the Development of Science and Technology (2006-2020) reinforces China's ambition to become a global technological power. China consciously is trying to transition from a manufacturing-based economy to an innovation and knowledge-based economy; progress towards this goal is already in evidence. Take the OECD statistics on China's R&D expenditures as an example. Regardless of whether they are $136 billion or $37 billion or, probably and more accurately, somewhere in between, there has been a trend of rising spending on R&D, and this trend will have positive implications for China's economic transition away from a heavy natural-resource-and-energy-using, environmentally destructive model of economic development. This suggests that the transition to a knowledge economy is not only good for China, but also for the rest of the world.

The plan's emphasis on indigenous innovation is not as protectionist as it seemed to some at first sight. Chinese leaders understand that in today's globalized world economy, lone ranger strategies will likely not be successful. Along with strengthening its own innovative capabilities, China also must become more adept at collaboration and cooperation. Obviously, for a range of economic, political, and national security reasons, China is eager to become a more innovation-oriented society, but only can achieve this goal by becoming more integrated into the global economy and transnational knowledge networks. The real challenge for China is how to effectively access and utilize global resources rather than to worry about becoming overly technologically dependent.

References

OECD (2006), OECD Science, Technology and Industry Outlook (Paris).

National Bureau of Statistics (NBS), China Statistical Yearbook (Beijing: China Statistics Press, various years.

National Bureau of Statistics and Ministry of Science and Technology (NBS/ MST), China Statistical Yearbook on Science and Technology (Beijing: China Statistics Press, various years).

National Bureau of Statistics (NBS) (2006), "Statistical Communiqué on the 2006 National Economy and Social Development of the People's Republic of China," available online at http://www.stats.gov.cn/english/newsandcomingevents/t20070301_402388091.htm (accessed March 1, 2007).

National Bureau of Statistics and Ministry of Science and Technology (NBS/ MST) (2006), 2006 China Statistical Yearbook on Science and Technology (Beijing: China Statistics Press), p. 107.

National Bureau of Statistics, National Development and Reform Commission, and Ministry of Science and Technology (NBS/NDRC/MST, 2006), 2006 China Statistical Yearbook on High Technology Industry (Beijing: China Statistics Press).

Serger, Sylvia Schwaag (2006), "China: From Shop Floor to Knowledge Factory?" In Magnus Karlsson (ed.), The Internationalization of Corporate R&D: Leveraging the Changing Geography of Innovation (Östersund, Sweden: IPTS), pp. 227-266.

Waldmeir, Patti (2006), "China Asserts Patent Rights in U.S. Court," *Financial Times*, October 22.

Research for this project was completed during several fieldwork trips in China during January 2006 to March 2007. Denis Fred Simon is Professor at the School of International Affairs at Penn State; Cong Cao is a Senior Researcher at the Levin Graduate Institute at the State University of New York; Richard P. Suttmeier is Professor of Political Science at the University of Oregon.

Restaurant Franchising in China

Ilan Alon
Vol.7 No.2
Spring 2008

Franchising is an operations strategy that works in various locations around the globe. It is essentially a contractual relationship between a franchisee and a franchisor trading rights and obligations. The franchisee has the right to market the brand and/or process of a franchisor in return for a fee and ongoing royalties. In the case of business-format franchising, the franchisor transfers both the know-how and the brand of the business, and often provides additional support. As firms internationalize, they face differences in operating environments, economics, politics and culture. Successful international franchising usually rests on the ability to transplant strategy that was successful in the home country.

Restaurant franchisors are flocking to invest in China for obvious reasons: 1.3 billion people, 230 million middle-class consumers (in 2005), the world's highest economic growth rate in the last 20 years, WTO membership, and favorable changes in recent franchise and contract laws. McDonald's, KFC, Burger King, Gold's Gym and Papa John's have already set up shop. And opportunities are not only in the restaurant sector. Across the service industries in China, which typically use franchising, growth abounds (real estate, retailing, hotels, etc.).

There is a dark side, however, to franchising in China. Franchising regulations have changed multiple times, creating an unstable environment for franchising contracts to proliferate. For example, the new regulations require a franchisor to open some stores and operate them before being able to sell franchise rights.

Secondly, the Chinese market is still not culturally used to franchising governance, including the lack of resolve to protect intellectual property rights. Franchising requires a high degree of trust and legal protection. Thus, one way to succeed in the Chinese market is to enter one of the major cities using company-owned outlets. In this way the franchisor can gain familiarity with the cultural, economic and legal environments. Gaining an understanding of the nuances of the local market can help a company assess the potential. This is what most of the large multinational chains, such as McDonald's, KFC and Yum, have done.

In China today, many of the global franchising companies have a small percentage of their total outlets franchised, while others have used it extensively even though they do not use franchising in their home market. Kodak, for example, wanted to create channels of distribution for its film and, thus, developed a quasi-franchising film-development retail model for Kodak Express in China, relying on the promise of franchisees to buy paper and equipment from Kodak. Royalties, per se, were not charged.

For those interested in investing in the China market, Shanghai is an excellent entry point because the government has helped the city become a magnet for economic growth. Shanghai offers numerous economic incentives, an increasingly westernized population, and a large number of tourists and expatriates. In addition, the per capita income in Shanghai is over $11,000 in purchasing power parity (Kwan, 2002), among the highest in mainland China.

There is also reason for caution here, however. While legal reforms have taken place, laws still seem archaic and sporadically enforced. There remains insufficient protection for copyright, trademark and intellectual property. Add the language barrier, the cultural distance between the West and China, and the fact that many Western brands are unknown in China, and it's clear that Shanghai is a challenging opportunity to be considered carefully.

In Shanghai, the fundamentals of successful restaurant franchising are similar to those in the west: consumers want flavorful food, delivered quickly and efficiently in a clean, pleasant environment at an affordable price. One recent survey of people in Shanghai conducted by the author revealed that consumers rated taste, service, atmosphere, price and brand name in declining order of importance when selecting a restaurant. Given the cultural, social, political and infrastructure differences in Shanghai, complete standardization is unlikely.

The key is to assess what adaptation will be necessary. The following considerations may be helpful.

Product - The product includes the novelty, service, atmospherics, and overall experience that the restaurant provides. Traditional domestic restaurants are not direct competitors. Franchisors may be more successful by emphasizing the "westernness" of their products, making standardization viable. Of course, minor modifications will be required to adapt to local tastes. For example, Starbucks in Shanghai offers a sausage Danish, and McDonald's serves seafood soup.

Promotion - Adaptation will depend largely on the product strategy. Standardized products make a standardized message possible, while different products mean different messages. Pizza Hut, for example, localized its business by decorating with large red "Double Happiness" signs, decorative firecrackers, traditional poetic couplets and the traditional Chinese character Fu (fortune); changing the design of the red roof to a Chinese feather calligraphy brush filled with red; and offering a customized "Xinyi" (goodwill) pizza from the Chinese New Year to the Lantern Festival.

Pricing - First-time visitors to Shanghai are amazed at the low prices of locally-made goods. International franchisors need not use local restaurant prices for reference. As long as the product is of high quality, and presents a new concept of consumption, a higher price will signal quality and credibility. Still, average income is substantially lower than in the West. Effective strategy might include portioning some products in sizes that can be purchased at very low price points. Both McDonald's and KFC ran 1 Yuan (about 12 cents) ice cream specials to entice customers into the store.

Distribution - Three location strategies seem viable.

- Downtown - The commercial and cultural center boasts the greatest variety of restaurants. But high rents have restricted growth. Only 2,100 of over 29,000 restaurants are located in Xuhui and Jing-an, the busiest sections and the center of the downtown area. Foreign restaurants are concentrated in Huaihai Lu, Maoming, Nan Lu and Henshan Lu – streets of the French Quarter in old Shanghai.

- Special Economic Zones - Pudong, a financial center and the site of many multinational corporations and government offices, has 2,700 restaurants. Substantial residential construction is also underway. Hongqiao, west of Shanghai, boasts over 1,300 restaurants and is a favorite area of expatriates and foreign investors.

- Upscale Residential - About 2 million people have moved to suburban residential areas, made possible by numerous infrastructure projects that have increased the commutability of city workers.

Target Markets - Three segments represent attractive targets for international restaurant franchisors.

- Foreigners and Expatriates - Short and long-term expatriates, visitors and tourists have relatively high income and a willingness to pay a premium for familiar food with consistent quality. Continued foreign investment will result in a growing expatriate population as well as an increase in tourism.

- Business People and Young Professionals - Includes educated professionals in the 25-50 age group. This group is likely to be the most receptive to new ideas, value the foreign dining experience, and possess sufficient discretionary income.
- Young Emperors - Preschool through college-age children. There are an estimated 1.25 million one-child families in Shanghai. "Young Emperors" command the attention of the extended family and have a substantial influence on family buying decisions. A foreign restaurant that attracts these children will attract their parents and extended family as well.

Restaurant franchisors that miss the opportunity to enter China now will face intense competition from early entrants. It will be difficult for restaurant franchisors entering now to beat the scale and profitability of the already entrenched McDonald's and KFC. Nonetheless, the market is vast and great potential exists in many niches.

Despite the potential, doing business in China is difficult. The language and culture are remarkably distinct. Franchisors should consider finding a local partner who can help them navigate the local business environment. A partner in the same industry with channels of distribution, industrial connections, and guanxi (personal connections) can greatly facilitate the success of the franchisor.

References:

Alon, Ilan and Dianne Welsh, eds. (2001), *International Franchising in Emerging Markets: China, India and Other Asian Countries*, Chicago IL: CCH Inc. Publishing.

Alon, Ilan (2007), "Master International Franchising in China: The Case of the Athlete's Foot," *International Journal of Entrepreneurship and Small Business*, 1 (4), 41-51.

Alon, Ilan and Ke Bian (2005), "Real Estate Franchising: The Case of Coldwell Banker Expansion into China," *Business Horizons*, 48 (3), 223-231.

Alon, Ilan, Mark Toncar, and Lu Le (2002), "American Franchising Competitiveness in China," Journal of Global Competitiveness, 10 (1), 65-83.

Kwan, Chi Hung (2002), "How Far is Coastal China Behind the Industrialized Countries?" available at http://www.rieti.go.jp/en/china/02080901.html.

"An Analysis Based on Purchasing Power Parity," (retrieved June 8, 2008): http://www.rieti.go.jp/en/china/02080901.html.

Ilan Alon holds the Cornell Distinguished Chair of International Business, and is the Executive Director of the China Center, at Rollins College, Winter Park, Florida.

Bridge Under Water:
The Dilemma of the Chinese Petition System

Qin Shao
Vol. 7 No. 1
Winter 2008

"Xinfang," or petitioning to authorities, has been one of the channels for the Chinese people to air grievances and seek justice since ancient times. But it has taken a new and disturbing shape in the current era of economic reform. In fact, there has been an ever intensifying, nationwide, though uncoordinated, active petition movement in China since the late 1980s. Economic reforms have generated tremendous tensions and corruption, and allowed more personal and political freedom. These changes have fostered an acute consciousness about one's own interests as separate from and in conflict with that of the state. These factors are in part responsible for the rise of the petition phenomenon. But the system is by and large broken. It has not only failed to ease tensions but also has become part of the problem, further contributing to heightened popular complaints.

The idea that aggrieved people could bring their complaints directly to higher authorities is rooted in ancient Chinese statecraft that defined a society ruled by man – that the benevolent and wise emperor and his upright, powerful officials would correct the wrongdoings of abusive, lower-ranking officials and return justice to the people once they learned about their suffering. It was meant to check local officials, connect the people with a sense of justice from above, and thereby reinforce the emperor's power and image.

The Chinese Communist Party launched its own petition system in 1951. The Party intended for it to serve as a bridge to closely link the government with the people by conveying the latter's concerns to relevant authorities for possible solutions. But under Mao, petitioning was infrequently used in individual, localized cases. The increasingly widespread use of this mechanism by the Chinese from remote corners to major urban centers is a new and unique phenomenon of the post-Mao era. But the various petition offices from the region to the center do not have any real power to directly solve any specific issues. The authorities that do possess power to resolve those issues are often the root cause of the complaints in the first place. In other words, rampant institutional corruption has both enabled and disabled the petition system. As such, the system has failed to protect the people and the bridge has been under water. As many cases have lingered for years and even decades and some people have turned into full-time "petition specialists," the system has become a trap that consumes enormous energy and resources of both the petitioner and the government without serving its stated purpose. This article takes a critical look at the petition system from the perspective of government regulations, the new trends in petitioning, and the perspective of the petitioner in an effort to provide some understanding about the current state of that system.

In October 1995 the State Council issued the "Regulations of Petition" with 44 items as a detailed nationwide guideline to respond to the mounting problems and pressures resulting from the reform. But new conflicts warranted almost immediate and ongoing update. Since then numerous documents and directives titled "petition specifics," "petition methods," "urgent notice on petition," and "rules on orderly petition" were issued on matters concerning the environment, labor, welfare, stock market, mine safety and many others by various government agencies in Beijing. Provincial and municipal governments have also issued their own rules.[1] The proliferation of petition-related documents testifies to the seriousness and persistence of the matter.

Not surprisingly, in 2005, the State Council issued a new version of the regulation with 51 items, 90 percent of which was either new or different as significant additions and revisions were made to the 1995 version.[2] In the meantime, books and pamphlets such as, "Supplemental Reading to 'Regulations of Petition'" and "Questions and Answers on 'Regulations of Petition'" were rushed to bookstores and classrooms of the nation's law schools.

The revisions of the 2005 Regulations served two purposes. One is to better "regularize," i.e. control, the petitioners; the other is to compel local officials to take more responsibility in dealing with petitions. The revisions tried to fix a system that was close to its break point. First of all, the official term "xinfang," defined as petition by "letter, e-mail, fax, telephone, and foot," is misleading.[3]

1   See a selected list of more than 30 such regulations issued between 1996 and 2005 in "Xin-fang tiaoli" yibentong (Comprehensive reading of "Regulations of Petition") (Beijing: Fazhi chubanshe, 2005), pp. 276-280.

2   Cao Kangtai and Wang Xuejun (eds.) Xinfang taoli fudao duben (Supplemental reading to "Regulations of Petition") (Beijing: Zhongguo fazhi chubanshe, 2005), pp. 15-21.

3   Cao and Wang (eds.) Supplemental Reading to "Regulations of Petition," p. 349.

Most petitioners use the term "shangfang"—in-person petition to higher authorities. The difference in terms reflects a significant gap between the government intention and the actual practice. While the government prefers written petitions and includes in its regulations "walk-in petition" as only one of the xinfang forms, people no longer believe that anything short of an in-person presence can resolve their cases. The 2005 revision of the Regulations of Petition was by and large prompted by the dramatic increase of in-person petition cases and also repeated petitions for the same cases. Such cases concentrated in five areas that include urban housing demolition and relocation, rural land seizure, health care, education, and the legal system. In recent years, official sources have consistently identified problems in these areas as the main contributors to heightened popular discontent and social instability in China. In the first eight months of 2004, for instance, various petition offices from the county to the central government levels witnessed 125 percent increase in such cases compared wtih the same period a year previous, of which 31 percent were repeated petitions for the same cases.[4]

The other alarming trend is the rise of group petitions, termed as "jifang" or "qunfang," which the government is most vehemently against as any collective action spells potential trouble. The number of people who were involved in group petitions increased more than 20 percent in the first eight months of 2004 compared to the same period in 2003. Also in 2004, the petition cases received by the county, district, province, and the state petition offices grew 11 percent, 14 percent, 17 percent, and 20 percent, respectively, forming a reversed pyramid. This scale shows the ineffectiveness of the local governments in dealing with popular grievances, which in turn puts great pressure on the various state petition offices in Beijing.

Over the years petitioners have often resorted to desperate tactics as their cases drag on for years and even decades. In an extreme case, in 1991 a peasant mother in Henan province lost her 20-year-old son to brutal beatings by the local police and mine bosses. After local authorities dismissed her case, she cut her son's head off and carried it all the way to Beijing. Thirteen years later, in 2004, she had been compensated a mere 5,000 Yuan and she was still petitioning. The local government, meanwhile, had reportedly spent 40,000 Yuan in efforts to stop her from petitioning.[5] The petitioners have also employed other radical means that have caused violent clashes with officials, such as occupying government offices, holding up official transportation, and blocking traffic.

More and more petitioners also choose to come to Beijing during important national festivals and events such as the National Day on October 1 and the annual "two meetings" in March of the National People's Congress and the People's

---

4　*Ibid. p. 16.*
5　*Qingnian cankao, 12 May 2004, pp. A13-14.*

Political Consultative Conference.[6] They protest outside those meeting places both to embarrass the government and in hopes of a chance meeting with an upright, powerful official who will magically set things right for them. The government has routinely rounded them up and sent them back to their hometowns, where some of them were beaten, detained, or put under house arrest. To better control the petitioners, the revised 2005 Regulations specify that petitioners are protected by law only when they go to designated offices at scheduled office hours, and that group representatives are limited to no more than five people. Further, those who continue with "abnormal petitions" are threatened with legal consequences.[7]

The nationwide petition movement, or more accurately, the nationwide failure of the petition system, has put the Party's claimed highest priority – social stability and harmony – at risk and caused grave concern to Beijing. The 2005 Regulations attempted to compel local officials to improve their dealings with petitioners to reduce the numbers of petitioners coming to the capital. The Regulations connect the performance of officials in handling petition cases with their overall assessment and threaten to punish failed cadres with legal and administrative procedures. The stated purpose is to assure that people receive the same treatment from local officials as from those in Beijing and that their problems would be solved locally.[8] The new Regulations also suggest new channels, such as e-mail and telephone, for petitioners, and broader social participation from lawyers and volunteers to help with the petition process.[9] These new measures were intended to provide some relief to the overburdened system and to control the scope of the petition movement.

But neither the new channels nor the legal threats are likely to ease the movement any time soon. The system is inherently flawed because the sources of popular grievance, namely rampant corruption, are deeply rooted in the institutions handling the petitions. How can the people expect the very local officials who abused them to serve them justice? Also, the petition system has itself become a reason for increased and repeated petitions because it often invites revenge. One study indicates that among the 632 petitioners surveyed, 56 percent of them kept petitioning because local government, as an act of retribution, attacked and even arrested people who petitioned persistently and thus caused them additional grievances.[10]

On the other hand, petitioning has gained a life of its own in other ways; it has become a ritual for the petitioners. Take Shanghai as an example, where in-person petitioning is most prevalent. The main municipal petition office is conveniently

---

6   *Cao and Wang (eds.) Supplemental reading to "Regulations of Petition," pp. 15-16.*

7   *Ibid. Pp. 19, 23, 27-30.*

8   *Ibid., p. 26.*

9   *Ibid., pp, 25, 351-52.*

10   *http://news.sina.com.cn/c/2004-11-17/15374946096.shtml.*

located downtown, on People's Square, with a central subway station and many bus stops nearby. There are also petition offices operated by other municipal organs, such as the Bureau of Urban Planning, and the Shanghai People's Congress, as well as by every district government. But the municipal petition office on the People's Square is the most popular. In cases of housing disputes involving eviction and loss of property, for instance, some of the residents would head to this office straight from their demolished homes, often carrying their elderly or sick family members on a stretcher, and others would come to show their fresh bruises and hospital records in the aftermath of a violent encounter with government-hired demolition teams.

Part of the attraction of this office, interestingly enough, is in the petitioners themselves. The office is open during the weekdays with Wednesday as the most crowded for those who have issues with demolition and relocation. They all come on Wednesday by a tacit agreement and form a kind of community with a shared plight and purpose.[11] Some of the residents had been full-time petitioners for more than a decade and earned a nickname of "petition specialists." There are also star petitioners among them who take it upon themselves to study relevant official documents and to come up with new strategies and demands. They are highly recognizable, and in fact, an institution at this petition office. While their demands have not been met, they have become unusually learned, experienced, and shrewd in dealing with the authorities, with much to offer to the newcomers. Collectively, these petitioners are well-informed, resourceful, and tenacious. Sometimes they are even more informed on government policies and regulations than the officials who receive them. Any newcomers who step into this office and get their "Petition 101" also feel energized and less alone. These petitioners learn from each other how to fight for their causes, keep each other up to date on new developments, share material, and draw strength from and support one another. The municipal petition office thus has become an unofficial gathering point and self-support center for the petitioners who have built and extended a fellowship there. That the petition office has turned into a politically charged institution of sociability with its own veteran clients is perhaps the most telling evidence of its failure.

Yu Jianrong, a Chinese social scientist specializing in rural development at the Academy of Chinese Social Sciences, has done an in-depth investigation of the petition system through surveys and other means, mainly because prominent among the petitioners are peasants. In late 2004 his officially sponsored research project produced a report that recommends the elimination of the petition system altogether. His argument is at once compelling and utterly obvious: the system simply does not work. Among the 2,000 cases he studied, only three of them were

---

11 *One person I interviewed is a retailer with her own shop and a flexible schedule, and she chose Wednesday as her day off so that she could go to the petition office.*

resolved, not due to the institutional mechanism but because certain important individuals and enlightened officials took an interest in those three cases. He further points out the inherent flaw in the petition system that renders it useless – the lack of necessary authority to resolve the issues brought to its offices. On the other hand, according to Yu, the petition system highlights the failure of the law and thus severely diminishes its authority, since it is the legal system that was supposed to deal with most of those issues. Related to that is the reinforcement of the notion that China continues to be a society ruled by man, not by law.[12] In short, Yu concludes that the petition system is not only useless, but also harmful.

Yu's research was part of the process the State Council initiated to review and revise the 1995 petition regulations. As the publication of the 2005 Petition Regulations indicates, the central government did not accept Yu's suggestion to abolish the petition system. In fact, his proposal caused a heated debate and was highly controversial in China, which is hardly surprising. With the continuous spread of corruption and the weak enforcement of the law, the petition system continues to at least channel popular complaints and give the illusion of hope to people – airing social grievances often helps defuse destructive emotions, and providing illusion is a way to sustain hope when the real thing is missing. That so many petitioners have patiently appealed their cases for years is a case in point. In other words, the petition system, while not solving those cases, has nevertheless helped absorb tensions generated by reforms, at least temporarily. Also, the thousands of officials and staff involved in the petition system depend on it for their positions and jobs. Many of the petitioners I talked to were convinced that those officials and staff were in no rush to solve their cases in order to preserve their own jobs.

Opposition to closing the petition system could also come from unlikely candidates, such as the petitioners themselves who have complained about and suffered from its failure. The meaning of petition for the petitioners is a subject that deserves more attention. Many of the petitioners have endured grave losses of loved ones, homes, land, jobs and other sources of livelihood, and any meaningful focus in life that was central to their material and emotional well-being. Their quotidian lives have been shattered, as has their sense of dignity, trust, justice, and faith in friendship, community, family, and government. Yet society has refused to even acknowledge their loss, and thus denied them the necessary space and opportunity to openly and legitimately mourn that loss. It was often out of utter despair that they embarked on a petition trip, which many of them refer to as "a road with no return," a reflection of both their determination to pursue justice to the very end and the ineffectiveness of the system.

To many of them, petition becomes not only a channel to seek justice but also an interactive ritual for mourning, a passage to restoring normalcy in life; at least

---

12 *http://news.sina.com.cn/c/2004-11-17/15374946096.shtml*

that is what they have hoped for. They also incorporate petition into their daily routines, and it has indeed become a new focus in their lives. On certain weekdays they go to visit local petition offices, and during certain times of the year, – March for instance – they go to Beijing. They have their own community, with friends and acquaintances to meet and chat with on petition trips and around the petition offices. In this long and miserable journey, some of them have given up hope but cannot admit to themselves that they have been defeated. They cannot afford to lose yet another focus in life. So they press on, for petitioning seems to be the only thing left to do, with or without a purpose. Asked about the idea of abolishing the petition system, one long-time petitioner answered with a question, "Then what do I do?" They have no alternative, much less a valid alternative; the petition system has become a trap from which they see no way out.

The epidemic of institutional corruption in China has created a dysfunctional petition system that leaves both parties involved—the government and the petitioner—frustrated but dependent on it and on each other. This co-dependence perpetuates a life of its own. The system will either be invalidated by a determined, thorough reform in the political machine to eliminate corruption or else it will erode the machine itself. Until then, the system will find abundant institutional debris to sustain its inertia and justify its existence as a futile but necessary measure in this transitional period of Chinese society.

Qin Shao is Professor of History at The College of New Jersey, Ewing, New Jersey.

Peking University and
the Centers for Disease Control:
A 25-Year U.S.-China Collaborative Project

Deborah Kowal
Vol. No.3
Fall 2007

We are all used to reading about tension and controversy between China and the United States. It seems a product made in China is recalled almost every day. Then there are disputes over intellectual property rights, and trouble over human rights, Taiwan and Tibet. The list goes on and on. Success stories tend to get less attention, even if they bring results that help alleviate human misery. This is one such story. Medical researchers from China and the U.S. have made quiet but notable progress in eliminating a range of particularly debilitating birth defects: spina bifida and other related congenital problems, which are known as neural tube defects.

> *When you want something to happen, you cannot give up. You need patience. So many foreigners come to China and think they can have a success because they have made contact once or twice. Nothing happens based on one meeting.* **Dr. Li Zhu**

This is a story that has unfolded over a quarter century, and it holds lessons for anyone from the outside who wants to deal successfully with China.

The China-U.S. Collaborative Project for Neural Tube Defect Prevention, under the auspices of the Beijing Medical University (BMU) and the U.S. Centers for Disease Control and Prevention (CDC), has achieved both scientific and operational success. First, the rate of neural tube defects in the Project sites in the high-risk northern provinces dropped 85 percent among the women who were at least 80 percent compliant in taking supplements containing a vitamin called folic acid. Even among women in the low-risk southern provinces, supplementation cut the rate by 40 percent. Second, the research team collected complete and clean data on 247,831 women and their pregnancies over the three years of the community intervention program. Forms were completed for 70 percent of the infants within one week of delivery and for all but a few percent within three months. With these numbers, the project became perhaps the largest community intervention study ever conducted, studying more than a quarter of a million women and their babies and relying on more than 16,000 health workers across 30 local counties and cities in five provinces. The rate of women lost-to-follow-up (5 percent) fell far below levels generally expected for studies of any kind. The collaborative project generated several notable articles, with the landmark study published in *The New England Journal of Medicine.*

The groundwork for the Project was forged in 1983, when a BMU professor of obstetrics and gynecology, Dr. Yan Renying, feared that too many babies were dying in Shunyi County, a suburb of Beijing. She requested technical assistance from the World Health Organization to guide her and her colleagues in conducting surveillance on infant deaths. WHO sent an epidemiologist who was on loan from the CDC: Dr. Brian McCarthy. He conducted several workshops so the clinicians and professors could learn the fundamentals of field and perinatal epidemiology.

One third of the deaths were due to neural tube defects, including conditions such as spina bifida. The incidence of the defects was 7.3 per 1,000 births. Dr. McCarthy wrote at the time, "To the writer's knowledge, this is the highest in the world and does not even represent the highest in the Beijing area." In one of Shunyi's townships, the rate of newborns born with any form of neural tube defect was astounding and tragic: Nearly 17 of every thousand infants had one of the defects—the highest in the world.

Neural tube defects pose a grave public health problem everywhere in the world, but they are particularly prevalent in many parts of China. Affluent nations such as the United States can provide surgical, medical, and physical therapy to help afflicted infants survive and eventually lead productive lives. Unfortunately, poorer nations such as China lack these therapeutic services. That lack of services, along with the strain on the families' finances, dooms these infants to early death, and frequently death while in utero. Their mothers and fathers suffer not only the loss of a pregnancy or child, but the ones who have a baby with the defect also bear a social stigma.

In 1983, Dr. Yan reported the findings to the public health world in the first annual Europe-China conference on perinatal health. At Dr. McCarthy's urging,

Standing in the dirt near their pig pen, the solemn-faced Chinese grandparents explain that the parents of a four-month-old baby girl with spina bifida have gone away. Her mother has run away, overcome with grief after having a child with a birth defect. Her father is out searching for his wife. The grandparents have not heard from them, and the baby still has no name. The moment is captured in a photograph that quickly and deeply tells the story of spina bifida and related birth defects in China.

—McKimmie M. China's Acid Test. *The West Australian*, June 25, 1994:1-2.

Dr. Godfrey Oakley, CDC's director of the Birth Defects Branch, attended the conference. After hearing Dr. Yan's presentation and looking over hospital logbooks that recorded infant deaths, Dr. Oakley pronounced, "China may have an epidemic of neural tube defects." Dr. Oakley had long been interested in finding ways to prevent spina bifida. At the time, the average cost for medical and surgical care for the surviving children born with spina bifida approached $100 million [US]. If the other costs of caring for these children are added, the total grew to $800 million. The heartache could not be put into monetary terms.

A substantial part of the difficulty in preventing spina bifida and similar defects was that the nervous system develops within a month after conception, before many women know they are pregnant. The other part of the difficulty was that medical researchers did not know what caused the defect. Was there something unusual about the women who lost pregnancies or delivered dead or deformed infants? Had any unusual event taken place that could have exposed the mothers and their fetuses to toxins? Did affected families pass on inherited problems? During the 1960s and 1970s, epidemiologists were just beginning to gather a body of evidence about the causes of birth defects. They suspected that some might be due to genetic abnormalities, but it would be three decades before the human genome project would produce enough information to give people hope of finding genetic keys to birth defects.

Dr. Oakley and his CDC colleagues were intrigued by the suggestion from earlier observations that vitamin deficiency might be involved, and had for several years been trying to find funding for a definitive clinical trial to look at the issue. Although CDC had great interest in finding effective ways to reduce the number of babies born with the condition, there were obvious barriers to launching a definitive clinical trial in the United States. Very small numbers of potential study cases meant it would take a decade or longer to find statistical significance; the costs of running a rigorous scientific study were high and growing higher; and it would be difficult to find comparison (control) cases among a population of women, who, upon hearing media reports of the study, could easily buy multivitamins on their own.

China, on the other hand, could provide a venue where a trial could be conducted at far lower cost and over a far shorter period of time, given the exceedingly high rate of neural tube defects. About one quarter of all such defects in the world were in China. China needed to manage its epidemic of neural tube defects, but it also sought to step boldly and rapidly into the modern age of science and technology. Together, Dr. Oakley and Dr. Yan agreed to work on a proposal that their two institutions join the search for ways to prevent these most common birth defects. It would take eight years of persuading superiors, finding funding, and calming the political suspicions, but eventually the collaborative project turned from proposal to reality.

At first, the project had all the ingredients for failure. The U.S. researchers were uncertain about the ability of the Chinese to conduct the rigorous trials that were coming to inform evidence-based medicine. In the early 1980s, the Chinese scientific community was just emerging from the effect of the national policies that closed them off from the rest of the world, causing their methodologies to lag behind their Western counterparts. Countless health professionals had been sent to rural outskirts during the Cultural Revolution, and the foundation of expertise remained thin even in the later 1980s when a fledgling project office housed at Beijing Medical University needed to find young epidemiologists, who had to learn many of their skills on the job.

In Atlanta, a CDC team faced the problem of how to coordinate massive fieldwork thousands of miles away. Tanks rolled into Tiananmen Square; for months, the Project appeared to be in jeopardy of termination. Some years later, U.S. jets mistakenly dropped bombs on the Chinese embassy in Belgrade, making the Chinese fear for the safety of U.S. researchers assigned to live in Beijing. The principal investigators in the BMU office faced pressures from mayors in the project counties, who pressed to get more of the tight research money as they pondered how they could produce the expected work with a shortfall of resources. The list of obstacles went on. China lacked telephones and electronic systems. Roads were bad. Education levels were low among the families who were to participate in the study. Delays took months, and sometimes years.

Managing the details in the field were two young epidemiologists: BMU's Dr. Li Zhu and CDC's Dr. Robert J. Berry. They shared a belief in what they felt were the critical underpinnings that allowed the Project's success: the right person in the right place; perseverance despite the obstacles; relationships developed over "walking a thousand miles" together; and sheer human capital.

The first principle of success was finding the 'right' people who knew how to build relationships, had drive, and shared a common work ethic. Every project needs a pivot point, someone who connects all the pieces. Dr. Li Zhu filled that role, linking Ministers of Health, university administrators, CDC researchers and chiefs, provincial and city and county leaders, medical directors, and staff. The American team, too, had some of the 'right people' who invested substantial time and effort. McCarthy, Oakley, and other CDC epidemiologists made dozens of visits to China. Dr. Berry and later Dr. Jacquelyn Gindler pulled up their households and lived in Beijing for several years, supervising the details of the Project's logistics and learning Chinese so that they could communicate directly with their colleagues.

Perseverance was the second reason for success. "When you want something to happen, you cannot give up. You need patience," Li Zhu explained.

> *"Think about it. We were successful because a lot of people went to the United States, and a lot of Americans came here. We had meeting after meeting. We worked together a long time, sometimes not knowing what would come of it. It has nothing to do with theories. You cannot find this kind of 'theory' in a book. If you want to do anything, you need to keep trying. Be patient, but insist that decisions be made. Chinese and Americans both talk about 'gritting your teeth.' You have to want to do what it is necessary for what you want, no matter how hard, no matter the difficulties and obstacles."*

The third underpinning of success was found in "friendships," both personal and professional, forged over years of detailed work. In building personal relationships, each team earned trust and learned to be trusting; respected each other's wisdom; and shared ownership not only of achievements, but also of frustrations. Everyone worked on working together. Berry reflected, "I think all the other relationships between bureaucracies and cultures are probably much less important than personal relationships. I didn't really understand that well when I went there."

The Project was a model for successful teamwork not only between professionals, but also between scientists and government officials. The research was supported by the government and conducted by the scientists. "During the long-term collaboration," said Dr. Li Zhu, "we faced a lot of problems and difficulties and obstacles. We always got together to discuss these challenges and think about solutions. I then talked with the Ministry of Health to find a solution from the China side and explained what I thought was the situation in the United States. My CDC colleagues worked on the U.S. side, and they could explain the Chinese situation."

Dr. Berry agreed. "From the beginning, we had the ability to sit down and decide what to do and, based on science, decide what should be done. The Chinese would get together and, because they were experienced within their own system, they did what needed to be done on their side. We did the same on our side."

Human capital came from the thousands of health workers throughout all levels of the health care system: hospital workers, clinic staff, registration officials, doctors, nurses, technicians, data-entry clerks, secretaries, drivers, and community service workers. A common opinion in the West is that developing countries, with workers who may have less training and little monetary reward for the added burden, cannot attain the accuracy and follow-up rates achieved in developed nations. However, no one had informed the young investigators, Drs. Li Zhu and Berry, that these were accepted limitations; instead, they sought the highest level of precise, accurate, and useful data.

"One of the things that really made this Project work," said Dr. Berry, "was that the counties were so engaged. In the beginning, little of what we were doing made sense to them, but we sent reports back to the counties to help them fix problems and it got people engaged in collecting data and making the data good." Local health officials traveled to their village clinics and township hospitals to track down information missing from the original data-collection booklets and forms. They kneeled over giant cross-tabulation tables laid across the floors of their offices to begin the detective work of finding the right matches, sometimes working most of the night. They worked on the floor, because that was the only space large enough to spread out one million surveillance cards.

As the Project achieved its stated goal to prevent spina bifida, it additionally achieved others. BMU developed institutional strength by fostering young, bright, hardworking scientists. The local Project sites grew capacity through the training and experience, expanding the expertise beyond the study's needs and into the realm of medical-care delivery and other types of medical research. The Project developed one of the largest databases in the world, which grows as the researchers continue to follow more than 200,000 families each year. The data collected are clean and complete; they are cited throughout the world. The surveillance system can track the potential long-term benefits from exposure to folic acid, of course, but in these records of mothers and children lie any number of answers for questions no one has yet thought to ask.

Deborah Kowal is a medical writer and editor based in Atlanta, Georgia.

Building a Comprehensive Strategy
for China's Environmental Clean-up

Baogang Guo
Vol.8 No.2
Spring 2009

Last year's Beijing Olympic Games witnessed a breathtaking makeover of the city's environment. Beijing's sky became blue almost overnight. Anyone who had visited the Chinese capital just a few months before would be amazed to find that the thick smog that hung over the city disappeared nearly completely, like a miracle. However, what they did not know was how much effort the Chinese government had put into the environmental clean-up in order to fulfill its promise to the International Olympic Committee (IOC) about environmental protection. It is estimated that China spent nearly $10 billion on improving Beijing's environmental quality. Many drastic measures were taken in the months prior to the Games. Coal-fired power stations in the city were converted to gas-burning stations. More than 1,400 old gas stations and 10 oil depots were closed down for good. Another 200 major polluting factories were ordered to shut down temporarily. Capital Iron and Steel, one of the largest steel makers in China, was ordered to relocate its mills to a new industrial park far away from the capital city. Car drivers were told to drive only on alternate days according to their cars' tag numbers. Despite these measures, the air remained foggy and unstable just a month before the games. The authorities ordered an expansion of the strict air-quality control measures to cities adjacent to Beijing and asked some of their heavy-polluting factories to shut down their production operations temporarily as well. As a result, during the first half of 2008, Beijing's sulfur dioxide emission level decreased nearly 13% compared with the same period of 2007. During the month of August, when the games were held, the air quality in Beijing was rated as excellent for almost half of the month, and the remaining days were rated as good.

These massive clean-up efforts are unparalleled in the history of the Olympic Games. They demonstrate not only the determination of the Chinese government to meet its Olympic obligations but also the ability of the authorities to use administrative muscle to fight pollution. After years of liberal reform, it is noteworthy that the state still has so much power at its disposal. This administrative capability is almost beyond imagination in a typical western democracy. However, the desire to present to the world a clean image is only part of the story. Since 2005, "scientific development" has become the new buzz phrase in China's political lexicon. Leaders in Beijing have apparently realized that the single-minded pursuit of economic growth at the expense of environmental and human development is not sustainable. Indeed, China has already paid a huge price for decades of neglect of its environment. In just a few decades, China quickly became one of the most polluted countries on earth. Air was filled with dirty particles, rivers and lakes became filthy and stinky, and underground water became undrinkable. Industrial pollution contributed greatly to the environmental nightmare. A report issued by the World Bank on China's environment points out that "many of China's waterways are close to biological death from excessive discharge of organic pollutants. In many urban areas, atmospheric concentrations of pollutants such as suspended particulates and sulfur dioxide routinely exceed World Health Organization safety standards by very large margins. Hundreds of thousands of people are dying or becoming seriously ill from pollution-related respiratory disease each year." As a result, sixteen Chinese cities were on the World Bank's most polluted city list, and Linfen City in Shanxi Province was cited as the world's most polluted city in 2007. The Chinese government has no choice but to develop a comprehensive strategy to toughen its environmental policy.

Beijing's clean-up prior to the Olympic Games followed the traditional "command-and-control" approach involving the identification of sources of environmental pollution, setting emission standards, inspecting for non-compliance, and forcing the shutdown of polluting factories. Since 2005, the State Environmental Protection Administration (SEPA) has launched several waves of an environmental "New Deal." On January 18, 2005, SEPA ordered 30 major construction projects, mostly new power plants, to suspend construction for lack of required environmental impact reports. Among the projects put on hold were the 12,600 megawatt Luoqi Du hydroelectric power station and the underground Hydroelectric Power Station connected with the Three Gorges Dam project. On January 27, 2005, SEPA launched another strike. This time, 46 existing power plants were ordered to install SO_2 reduction devices within a fixed time period. Three subsequent "storms" followed. On February 7, 2006, SEPA announced that it would inspect 127 chemical projects. On January 7, 2007, SEPA used a regional ban on new investment projects against four cities and four enterprises for their violations of some regulatory requirements. On July 3, 2007, SEPA put the ban on new projects for six cities, two counties and five industrial parks to punish them for pollution flowing into the Yangtze, Yellow, Huai and Hai rivers. This new power of "limiting approval of area development projects" gave the state environmental agency and local environmental protection bureaus veto power on new construction projects.

Aside from taking these drastic administrative measures, Chinese environmental regulators are also actively seeking a new market approach that emphasizes the use of incentives such as emission quotas, pollution levies, emissions trading, green credits, green capital markets, ecological compensation, and environmental liability insurance to force enterprises to comply with environmental standards. This approach calls for an active role of the state in the creation of a system of environmental economy but not for direct interference with business decisions. Since 2008, the government has shifted its focus from punishing polluters to institution building. As part of the environmental "New Deal," SEPA introduced a number of new systems to help enterprises and consumers deal with environmental disputes. First, SEPA issued a circular about liability insurance on environmental pollution. The hope is that the insurance system can help enterprises deal with monetary compensation in cases of environmental disaster without causing too much financial burden on an enterprise. The system also is designed to help protect the interests of victims and prevent the government from having to pay compensation in pollution cases. A pilot program has been implemented in several provinces. It is hoped that by 2015 the trial will be completed, and the system will be promoted nationwide.

Second, SEPA has initiated a new pilot project on emissions trade. The concept of emissions trade was introduced to China by Dr. Daniel Dudek, the chief economist of the American-based Environmental Defense Fund. In September 1999, the Fund signed an agreement with SEPA to complete a pilot project on total emissions control (TEC) and emissions trading under the framework of Sino-U.S. cooperation. Benxi and Nantong were selected as the first demonstration cities. In September 2001, the first sulfur dioxide emissions trade was successfully completed in Nantong, Jiangsu Province. In March 2002, SEPA and the fund cooperated in launching the "4+3+1" project in collaboration with the China Hua Neng Group. This project was an endeavor to initiate an integrated TEC and emissions trading policy in Shandong, Shanxi, Jiangsu and Henan provinces, and the cities of Shanghai, Tianjin and Liuzhou. Each of the jurisdictions completed quota allocations, trading regulations and policy demonstrations. In December 2007, Jiaxing city in Zhejiang Province established China's first emissions trading center. Beijing and Tianjing are in the process of setting up the nation's first carbon trading centers. Shanghai and Beijing have also established Environmental Energy Exchanges.

Additionally, the Chinese government is beginning to incorporate cooperative governance into its grand strategy of environmental regulation. This approach emphasizes transparency of decision making and participation by civic organizations. In 2004, SEPA issued a circular on the administrative-hearing process regarding environmental protection issues. The scope of the hearings can cover small, medium and large projects that have an impact on the environment. In 2005, the Beijing government decided to invest 30 million Yuan ($4 million) to install plastic at the bottom of a lake at Yuanmin Yuan, the remains of the Qing Dynasty imperial garden widely known as the Summer Palace, in order to prevent water leakage and save money. SEPA responded to the public criticism of the project by calling the first public environmental hearing on April 13, 2006. Seventy-three representatives were allowed to attend the hearing. Many of them were professors and experts. Several representatives from non-governmental organizations (NGOs) also appeared in the hearing. SEPA eventually decided to order the project to uninstall the finished anti-filtration plastic film at the lake.

Beginning in 1998, the World Bank and SEPA established GreenWatch, a public disclosure program for polluters. It uses the Environmental Performance Rating and Disclosure System to rate firms' environmental performance from the best to the worst in five colors—green, blue, yellow, red and black. The ratings are disseminated to the public through the media. The pilot program was initially tried in Zhenjiang, Jiangsu Province, and Hohhot, Inner Mongolia, with funds from a grant from the Bank's Information for Development Program. After pilot GreenWatch projects proved successful in 22 Chinese municipalities in seven provinces, the Chinese national government decided in November 2006 to extend the program to every city in the country by 2010.

Environmental NGOs and activists have played a role in this area as well. Currently, there are about 2,000 registered environmental groups in China. Many more are probably unregistered. A good example of cooperation among government, NGOs, entrepreneurs and citizens is Alxa's sandstorm treatment project. Alxa is located in the west of Inner Mongolia, which is the main source of China's sandstorms in northern China. The ecological deterioration in the area has threatened the livelihood of more than 196,000 herdsmen and created many ecologically displaced persons. On June 5, 2004, 100 Chinese entrepreneurs pledged to donate 100 million Yuan ($14 million US) to the Environmental Protection Public Welfare Fund to Control Sandstorms. The Alxa SEE Ecological Association was established, based on this initiative. The SEE Ecological Association has engaged in several pilot projects, including the "alternative energy and natural haloxylon woods zone protection" project and the "improving the sustainability of ALEXA ecological migrants" project. Its investment model calls for multilateral cooperation on the part of the association, government agencies, herdsmen, entrepreneurs, and international organizations. The government of Alxa Meng (Meng is an administrative unit used in Inner Mongolia) launched a "migration and transfer, centralized development" project to relocate herdsmen from Helan Mountain and Tengger to Barunbielli Town of Alxa and built 100 greenhouses for them. The SEE Ecological Association was invited to be a partner of this project, and provided technology training to herdsmen and support for the relocation.

International non-governmental organizations (INGOs) also have been closely cooperating with the Chinese government in recent years in the area of environmental protection. Since the mid-1990s, the number of international NGOs and philanthropic foundations conducting or funding environmental conservation campaigns has grown at an extraordinarily rapid pace. While the number of INGOs with offices in China has grown slowly, the size and resources of these offices has grown dramatically since 2000. The World Wildlife Fund, for example, has worked constructively with government officials at various levels to protect pandas and other endangered species, to preserve ecologically sustainable development, and to promote environmental education. It currently has over 40 projects in many provinces. In recent years, another U.S.-based INGO, the Nature Conservancy, has been invited to help guide a nationwide assessment of China's conservation priorities and help manage over 50 of China's 2,400 natural reserves because of its successful partnership with the Chinese government.

In January 2007, under the instruction of SEPA, the China Environmental Culture Promotion Association compiled and released its first environmental protection index. The index is intended to reflect public sentiment on environmental protection. China's first corporate responsibility index focused on the environment, called the Taida Environmental Index, was released on January 3, 2008. Forty listed companies from 10 environment-related industries compiled the index. As the first social responsibility index for China's capital market, the index is mainly aimed at evaluating listed companies' social responsibilities. Companies with a strong focus on social responsibility will be heralded by government and are likely to gain more opportunities for sustainable development.

To strengthen the administrative capacity of environmental regulation, the Chinese National People's Congress recently elevated SEPA to the Ministry of Environmental Protection (MEP). As one of five new super ministries, MEP's responsibility, departments and staff all significantly increased. From command-and-control strategy to market-based environmental economics, and from state governance to cooperative governance, the recently passed regulatory policies in China represent a new direction in China's environmental protection. It mirrors a fundamental shift in China's developmental strategy. The combined efforts should help produce some significant improvements in China's environment in years to come. One thing is clear: in the prolonged battle against environmental degradation, the state is no longer the monolithic actor, and the decision-making process has become more open, with a greater degree of civic participation. These changes could help foster a participatory culture in China and teach people how to be a partner in the governing process.

References:

Susmita Dasgupta, Hua Wang and David Wheeler, *Surviving Success: Policy Reform and Future of Industrial Pollution in China*, World Bank Policy Research Working Paper No.1856 (Washington D.C.: World Bank, February 1997): 2.

Han Lin, "SEPA Suspended 30 Projects for Violating Environmental Regulations," China.com.cn, January 18, 2005, http://big5.china.com.cn/chinese/huanjing/763371.htm (accessed on June 18, 2008).

Beijing Morning News, February 2, 2007.

Qi Jianrong, "Can Green Insurance be a good solution?" *Legal Daily*, February 19, 2008.

Environmental Defense in China, *China Emission Trading*, http://www.cet.net.cn (accessed on June 29, 2008).

People.com.cn, April 13, 2005.

SEE, ALXA SEE Ecological Association: Duty and Dream.

C. Chad Futrell, "Evolution of International NGOs in China: broadening environmental collaboration and shifting priorities" in Yang Dongping ed., *China's Environment Yearbook: Changes and struggles*, Vol. 2 (Brill Academic Publishers, 2008): 225-257.

Dr. Baogang Guo is Associate Professor of Political Science at Dalton State College, Dalton, Georgia .

About the Editors

Penelope B. Prime: Beginning with her first visit to China in 1976, Penelope Prime has more than 30 years of experience studying the dynamic Chinese economy. After majoring in Chinese studies and studying Mandarin as an undergraduate, she earned a Ph.D. in economics at the University of Michigan. Dr. Prime is currently Professor of Economics in the School of Economics & Business at Mercer University in Atlanta teaching international economics and business in the MBA and Executive programs, and Director of the China Research Center. Dr. Prime's research focuses on China's economy and business environment, including topics such as China's foreign trade and investment, domestic market reforms, and provincial and local-level development, as well as applied business and economics cases on China and Asia. Her most recent book is *Global Giant: Is China Changing the Rules of the Game?*, co-edited with Eva Paus and Jon Western (Palgrave Macmillan, 2009).

James R. Schiffman: Mr. Schiffman is a Chief Copy Editor at CNN International, currently involved in various editorial and management issues including network style, hiring, and training. Mr. Schiffman currently is the primary editor for CNN International's "World News Asia" programs, which are broadcast in prime time in Asia. As a former correspondent in Beijing of the Asia Wall Street Journal, Mr Schiffman reported extensively on Chinese economic reforms, the role of foreign investment, and Chinese politics and culture at a time of rapid change and turmoil. Mr. Schiffman speaks Mandarin Chinese, and lectures frequently to academic and community groups. He also is pursuing a Ph.D. in Communication at Georgia State University, with an emphasis on media in China and is the editor of China Currents, the online journal of the China Research Center.